NUTSHELLS

EVIDENCE
IN A
NUTSHELL

AUSTRALIA
Law Book Company
Sydney

CANADA and USA
Carswell
Toronto

HONG KONG
Sweet & Maxwell Asia

NEW ZEALAND
Brookers
Wellington

SINGAPORE and MALAYSIA
Sweet & Maxwell Asia
Singapore and Kuala Lumpur

NUTSHELLS

EVIDENCE IN A NUTSHELL

FOURTH EDITION

by

Christina McAlhone

and

Dr Michael Stockdale,
Senior Lecturers in Law,
University of Northumbria
at Newcastle

London • Sweet & Maxwell • 2005

Published in 2005 by Sweet & Maxwell Limited of
100 Avenue Road, London, NW3 3PF
Typeset by LBJ Typesetting Ltd of Kingsclere
Printed in Wales by Creative Print and Design Group

No natural forests were destroyed to make this product.
Only farmed timber was used and re-planted.

A CIP catalogue record for this book is available
from the British Library.

ISBN 0 421 891 300

CONTENTS

1. BURDEN AND STANDARD OF PROOF

In legal proceedings, whether civil or criminal, it is necessary to determine which party has the burden of proving the facts in issue and what standard of proof is required.

CIVIL PROCEEDINGS

Burden of proof

In civil proceedings, the position is essentially that the party who raises an issue bears the legal burden of proof, *i.e.* the burden of proving the facts in issue (*Wakelin v London and South Western Railway* (1886)). Thus, for example, if the claimant asserts that he and the defendant formed a contract and that he suffered loss in consequence of the defendant's breach, it is for the claimant to prove that the contract was formed, that it was breached by the defendant and that he did suffer loss in consequence of that breach.

What is the effect of the defendant denying the claimant's assertions? If the defendant merely denies the claimant's assertions, this does not impose a burden of proof upon the claimant. Thus, for example, if the defendant claims that no contract was ever formed between himself and the claimant it is still the claimant who is required to prove the existence of the contract and not the defendant who is required to establish its non-existence. The claimant may fail to satisfy the burden of proof imposed upon him even if the defendant adduces no evidence and even though defence counsel does not cross-examine the claimant's witnesses. As a matter of sensible tactics, however, the defendant will normally do all that he can to rebut the claimant's case, where appropriate both cross-examining the claimant's witnesses and calling his own.

What is the position where the defendant raises an issue? Where the defendant puts forward a defence which goes beyond a mere denial of the claimant's case and actually raises new issues which the claimant did not raise, then the defendant does bear the burden of proving the relevant facts in issue. For example, if the defendant claims that the contract which he made with the claimant was frustrated, it is for him to prove that a frustrating event made its performance illegal or impossible. In such circumstances the defendant's assertion does not impose a burden of proof on the claimant, though, again, as a matter of sensible tactics, the claimant will normally do all that he can to negate the defendant's defence.

Does the concept of burden of proof become more important where there is little or no evidence in relation to an issue? Where there is little or no evidence in relation to an issue, the court may be unable to determine which version of the facts is correct. In such circumstances, the party who bears the legal burden of proof in relation to the relevant issue must have failed to satisfy it.

At times it may be unclear where the legal burden of proof lies with regard to an issue in relation to which little or no evidence is available. In such circumstances, when the court determines where the legal burden of proof lies it may also effectively be deciding the case before it. For example, in *Joseph Constantine Steamship Line Ltd v Imperial Smelting Corporation Ltd* (1942), the House of Lords was required to consider whether, where a defendant had raised the defence of frustration, he was merely required to prove that a frustrating event had taken place or whether the defence failed unless the defendant also proved that the frustrating event was not his fault. The case concerned the loss of a ship and there was little evidence before the court in relation to the issue of fault. If the burden of proving absence of fault fell on the defendant, then it would be difficult or impossible for defendants to maintain the defence in such circumstances. Conversely, if the burden of proving fault in order to negate the defence of frustration fell on the claimant, then, in such circumstances, the defence of frustration would, potentially, be available to defendants. The House of Lords, for a variety of reasons, held that the burden of proving fault lay on the claimant.

Standard of proof

The standard of proof in civil proceedings is proof on the balance of probabilities. Thus, the evidence adduced by the party who bears the legal burden of proof must persuade the judge (or the jury where, exceptionally, the claim is tried by a jury) that it is more probable than not that the facts were as that party asserts (*Miller v Minister of Pensions* (1947)). Consequently, where the evidence before the court equally supports the version of the facts put forward by the party who bears the legal burden of proof and the version put forward by the other party, the party who bears the legal burden of proof has failed to satisfy it (*Wakelin v London and South Western Railway*). Equally, even though the evidence adduced by the party who bears the legal burden of proof is more persuasive than that adduced in rebuttal by the other party, the party who bears the legal burden of proof still fails to satisfy it if the evidence which he adduces does not persuade the judge that his version of the facts is more probably true than not (*Rhesa Shipping Co SA v Edmunds* (1985)).

Exceptionally, the standard of proof required in civil proceedings may be the criminal standard of proof, namely, proof beyond reasonable doubt. This may be the case either where this higher standard of proof is required in civil proceedings by statute or where the common law exceptionally so requires. Thus, for example, it appears that the criminal standard of proof is required in order to prove contempt of court in civil proceedings (*Re Bramblevale Ltd* (1970)).

Finally, it appears that where criminal conduct is alleged in civil proceedings the requisite standard of proof remains the civil standard, not the criminal standard (*In Re H and Others (Minors) (Sexual Abuse: Standard of Proof)* (1996)). Even so, it should be noted that, in practice, the more serious the allegation with which a civil court is faced, the more difficult it will be for the party who bears the burden of proving the truth of that allegation to persuade the court of the probability of its truth (*In Re H and Others (Minors) (Sexual Abuse: Standard of Proof)*. Indeed, in relation to the making of anti-social behaviour orders, it appears that, in order to achieve consistency in their decisions, magistrates should apply the criminal standard of proof (*R. (on the application of McCann) v Manchester Crown Court* (2002)).

CRIMINAL PROCEEDINGS

Burden of proof

In criminal proceedings, the position is essentially that, subject to limited exceptions, the legal burden of proof lies on the prosecution (*Woolmington v DPP* (1935)). Thus, for example, if the accused is charged with murder, it is for the prosecution to prove that the accused unlawfully killed the victim with malice aforethought.

What is the effect of the accused denying part or all of the prosecution's case? If the accused merely denies part or all of the prosecution's case, this does not impose a burden of proof upon the accused. Thus, for example, if the accused claims that he did not kill the victim, it is still the prosecution who is required to prove that the accused did kill the victim and not the accused who is required to prove that he did not. The prosecution may fail to satisfy the burden of proof imposed upon it even if the accused adduces no evidence and even though his counsel does not cross-examine prosecution witnesses. As a matter of sensible tactics, however, the accused will normally do all that he can to rebut the prosecution's case, where appropriate both cross-examining prosecution witnesses and calling his own witnesses.

What is the position where the accused raises an issue? Where the accused puts forward a defence which goes beyond a mere denial of the prosecution's case and actually raises new issues which the prosecution did not raise, then, even so, the accused will not normally bear the legal burden of proving the relevant facts in issue. Rather, provided that there is some evidence before the court upon which a properly directed jury would be entitled to find that the accused's defence was established, the normal rule is that the legal burden of rebutting the defence lies on the prosecution.

In other words, in such circumstances, the accused may be said to bear the "evidential burden" of adducing sufficient evidence to raise the defence, but if sufficient evidence to raise the defence is before the court then the prosecution bears the legal burden of disproving it. In reality, however, even if the evidence adduced by the accused fails to raise such a defence, the trial judge should still leave the defence to the jury if it is raised by evidence adduced by other parties (*e.g.* by evidence given by prosecution witnesses) (*R. v Bullard* (1957)). Thus, for example, if, upon a charge of murder, the accused claims that he was provoked, if the evidence before the court raises the defence of provocation, it is for the prosecution to prove that the accused was not provoked, not for the accused to prove that he was (*R. v Mancini* (1942)).

In what circumstances does the accused bear the burden of proving facts in issue? The accused bears the legal burden of establishing the common law defence of insanity (*McNaghten's Case* (1843)). Otherwise, the accused only bears the legal burden of proving facts in issue if this is imposed upon him by statute. For example, s.2(2) of the Homicide Act 1957 expressly places the legal burden of proving diminished responsibility on the accused.

Where a statute does not expressly place the legal burden of proving facts in issue upon the accused, it may do so by implication, though a judge should not readily infer that a statutory provision is of this effect (*R. v Hunt* (1987)). Essentially, it appears that where statute prohibits conduct of a certain type other than in specified exceptional circumstances, it will be for the accused to prove that he falls within the relevant exception (*R. v Edwards* (1975)). Whether a statutory provision does have this effect, however, fundamentally depends upon the construction of its specific provisions (*R. v Hunt*).

Thus, for example, where an accused is charged with selling liquor without a licence, the prosecution, in order to succeed, are merely required to prove that the accused sold liquor and are not required to prove that, at the time of the sale, the accused did not possess a licence (*R. v Edwards*). Rather, if the accused wishes to rely upon the possession of a licence in answer to the case against him, it is for him to prove that he did possess one at the relevant time.

[*Note:* s.101 of the Magistrates' Court Act 1980 provides, essentially, that where an accused relies upon such an exception in summary proceedings, the burden of proving the exception lies upon him. This provision effectively equates with the common law position encountered in relation to trial on indictment (*R. v Hunt*).]

Does the concept of burden of proof become more important where there is little or no evidence in relation to an issue? Where there is little or no evidence in relation to an issue, the court may be unable to determine which version of the facts is correct. In such circumstances, the party who bears the legal burden of proof in relation to the relevant issue must have failed to satisfy it.

In *R. v Edwards* (considered above), neither party had adduced evidence to prove that the accused did or did not possess a licence to sell intoxicating liquor. Thus, if the legal burden of proving that the accused did not possess such a licence had fallen on the prosecution, then the prosecution would have failed to prove an essential ingredient of its case. As was noted above, however, the Court of Appeal held that it was for the accused to prove that he did possess a licence if he wished to rely upon such possession in answer to the case against him.

Where a party to criminal proceedings bears the legal burden of proving facts in issue it is for the jury (or the magistrates in the context of summary trial) to determine whether the party has proved the relevant issue to the standard required by law. Normally, the jury will decide whether the party has satisfied the burden of proof following consideration of all of the relevant evidence (both that adduced by the prosecution and that adduced by the defence). At times, however, following completion of the prosecution's case, the accused may submit that there is no case for him to answer. In such circumstances, if the prosecution has not adduced sufficient evidence to raise a prima facie case then the judge will withdraw the case or, as appropriate, the relevant count, from the jury (*R. v Galbraith* (1981)). The prosecution may be said to have failed to satisfy the "evidential burden" (*i.e.* the burden of adducing sufficient evidence to entitle a properly directed jury to make a finding on the prosecution's behalf).

Standard of proof

Where the legal burden of proof lies on the prosecution, the standard of proof in criminal proceedings is proof beyond reasonable doubt. In other words, if there is more than a remote possibility of the accused's innocence, then he should be found not guilty (*Miller v Minister of Pensions*). Another way of expressing this standard of proof is to state that the jury must be "satisfied so that they feel sure" of the accused's guilt (*R. v Summers* (1952)).

Where the legal burden of proof lies on the accused, the standard of proof in criminal proceedings is proof on the balance of probabilities (*R. v Carr-Briant* (1943)).

Human rights

The presumption of innocence is embodied in Art.6(2) of the European Convention on Human Rights. Thus, where statute or the common law imposes a legal burden of proof upon the accused, this is capable of giving rise to a violation of Art.6(2).

The only common law defence which imposes a legal burden of proof upon the accused is the defence of insanity, and the Commission of Human Rights held (in *H v UK* (1990)) that requiring the accused to prove this defence did not give rise to a violation of Art.6(2).

In relation to the statutory imposition of a legal burden of proof upon the accused, whether or not this results in a violation of Art.6(2) will depend upon whether the statutory requirement, requiring the accused to prove the relevant facts in issue, falls within reasonable limits *(Salabiaku v France* (1988)). Thus, it appears that there will be no violation of Art.6 in circumstances in which statutory derogation from the presumption of innocence is justified and imposing a legal burden of proof upon the accused is proportionate (*R. v Lambert* (2001)). In circumstances in which imposing a legal burden of proof upon the accused would result in an Art.6 violation, however, it appears that the effect of s.3(1) of the Human Rights Act 1998 in this context is that the court must "read the statutory provision down" such that the accused is only required to satisfy an evidential burden in order to satisfy the statutory requirement, the legal burden of proof being borne by the accused (*R. v Lambert*).

In considering whether a statutory requirement which imposes a legal burden of proof upon the accused does fall within reasonable limits, it is necessary to consider matters such as: whether the statutory requirement requires the accused to disprove an essential element of the offence with which he is charged; the purpose of requiring the accused to prove the relevant fact in issue; how difficult it will be for the accused to prove the relevant fact in issue; the potential consequences for the accused if he is found guilty of the offence with which he is charged; the accused's rights; whether requiring the accused to prove the relevant fact in issue achieves a fair balance between the public interest and the protection of the human rights of the individual; and Parliament's view concerning what is in the public interest (*R. v DPP Ex p. Kebilene* (1994)). Thus, for example, in *R. v Ali; R. v Jordan* (2000), the Court of Appeal held that the statutory imposition of the legal burden of proving the defence of diminished responsibility on the accused, by s.2(2) of the Homicide Act 1957, did not give rise to a violation of Art.6(2) because s.2(2) did not require the accused to disprove an element of the offence of murder and it would be very difficult for the prosecution to disprove that defence if the legal burden of so doing was borne by the prosecution. In contrast, in *R. v Lambert*, the House of Lords, applying s.3(1) of the Human Rights Act 1998, held that the burden imposed upon the accused by the defence created by s.28(2) of the Misuse of Drugs Act 1971, concerning the accused's knowledge of matters alleged by the prosecution, was only an evidential burden, the prosecution bearing the legal burden of disproving the defence if evidence sufficient to raise it was before the court. The s.28(2) "defence" concerned an essential element of the offence with which the accused was charged (his knowledge of the matters alleged against him), if the accused was found guilty the maximum sentence was life imprisonment and, whilst it might be difficult for the prosecution to disprove the defence, requiring the accused to prove the defence was a disproportionate response to this difficulty.

2. COMPETENCE AND COMPELLABILITY

Most persons are both competent to give evidence in civil or criminal proceedings and can be compelled to do so. In this chapter we will consider those exceptional classes of person who either are not competent witnesses (*i.e.* persons who cannot give evidence) or who, whilst competent witnesses, are not compellable (*i.e.* persons who may choose to give evidence but cannot be required to do so).

CRIMINAL PROCEEDINGS

As regards the issue of competence, the general rule in criminal proceedings is that, under s.53(1) of the Youth Justice and Criminal Evidence Act 1999, all persons are competent to give evidence. In relation to compellability, the general rule is that a witness who is competent is also compellable. The remainder of this part of the current chapter is concerned with exceptions to these general rules.

The accused

Can the accused testify for the prosecution? Section 53(4) of the Youth Justice and Criminal Evidence Act 1999 provides that the accused is not a competent prosecution witness. Indeed, where several persons are charged in the proceedings, none of them are competent to give evidence for the prosecution. Thus, if A and B are charged in the same proceedings, neither A nor B are competent to give evidence for the prosecution. The effect of s.53(5) is, however, that B is competent (and may be compelled) to give evidence for the prosecution against A if B is no longer liable to be convicted. This will be the case if B pleads guilty, if B has already been acquitted of the relevant charge or charges or if the proceedings against B have been discontinued. Moreover, B may be compelled to give evidence for the prosecution against A if A and B are being tried separately.

Can the accused be a defence witness?   The accused is a competent defence witness but cannot be compelled to give evidence (Criminal Evidence Act 1898, s.1). Thus, if A and B are tried in the same proceedings, B may choose to give evidence for the defence but cannot be compelled to do so by A. If an accused does not testify in his own defence, however, the court may be entitled to draw an inference from his silence (see Chapter 4 below).

The spouse of the accused

The competence of the accused's spouse (husband or wife, not unmarried partner (*R. v Pearce* (2002))) in criminal proceedings is governed by s.53 of the Youth Justice and Criminal Evidence Act 1999. The compellability of the accused's spouse is governed by s.80 of the Police and Criminal Evidence Act 1984.

Can the accused's spouse testify for the prosecution? Under s.53(4) of the 1999 Act (considered above), the accused's spouse is not competent to give evidence for the prosecution if the spouse is charged with an offence in the proceedings. Since the spouse is not competent in such circumstances the spouse, of course, cannot be compelled to testify (Police and Criminal Evidence Act 1984, s.80(4)).

Even if the accused's spouse is competent to give evidence for the prosecution (*i.e.* where the spouse is not charged with an offence in the proceedings), the effect of s.80(2A)(b) of the 1984 Act is that the spouse can only be compelled to give evidence for the prosecution if the offence charged is of a type specified by s.80(3) of the 1984 Act (for example, if it involved an assault on the spouse or on a person under the age of 16 or if it is a sexual offence alleged to have been committed in respect of a person under the age of 16). In such circumstances, the spouse can only be compelled to give evidence in respect of the specified offence.

Can the accused's spouse be a defence witness? The accused's spouse is competent to give evidence for the defence (both for the accused and for any other persons charged in the same proceedings). Under s.80(2) of the 1984 Act, the accused's spouse may be compelled to give evidence for the accused unless the spouse is charged with an offence in the proceedings (in which case the effect of s.1(1) of the Criminal Evidence Act 1898 and of s.80(4) of the 1984 Act, both considered above, is that the spouse will not be compellable).

The effect of s.80(2A)(b) of the 1984 Act is that the accused's spouse may be compelled to give evidence for a person charged in the same proceedings as the accused (*i.e.* to give evidence for the accused's co-accused) only if the offence charged is of a type specified by s.80(3) of the 1984 Act (see above). In such circumstances, the spouse can only be compelled to give evidence in respect of the specified offence. Moreover, under s.80(4) of the 1983 Act and s.1(1) of the 1898 Act (both considered above), the accused's spouse is not compellable to give evidence for a person charged in the same proceedings as the accused if the spouse is charged with an offence in the proceedings.

Former spouses and spouses who refuse to testify

Section 80(5) of the 1984 Act provides that a former spouse of the accused is competent and compellable as if the accused and the former spouse had never been married. Finally, s.80A of the 1984 Act provides that the prosecution cannot comment upon the failure of the accused's spouse to testify.

Persons who cannot understand questions or give answers which can be understood

In criminal proceedings, under s.53(3) of the Youth Justice and Criminal Evidence Act 1999, a person will not be competent if it appears to the court that the person cannot both understand questions put to him and give answers to those questions which can be understood. Whether the issue of the competence of a witness is raised by the court or by one of the parties, s.54 of the 1999 Act provides that the party who called the witness bears the burden of proving on the balance of probabilities that the witness is competent. Section 54 also provides that proceedings to determine the competence of a witness will take place in the absence of the jury, that expert evidence may be received for the purpose of determining the witness's competence and that any questioning of the witness for this purpose will be conducted by the judge. Finally, s.54 provides that where the court gives or intends to give a special measures direction (see Chapter 5 below) in relation to a witness, the court must take this into account when determining the witness's competence.

Sworn and unsworn evidence

Section 55(2)(a) of the Youth Justice and Criminal Evidence Act 1999 provides that a witness under the age of 14 may not give sworn evidence in criminal proceedings. Moreover, under s.55(2)(b), a witness aged 14 or more may not give sworn evidence in criminal proceedings if the witness does not sufficiently appreciate the solemnity of the occasion and the particular responsibility of telling the truth which taking an oath involves. Section 55(3) provides that if a witness is able to give intelligible testimony (*i.e.* is able to understand questions and to give answers which can be understood (s.55(8)), the witness is presumed to sufficiently appreciate the above-mentioned matters unless evidence to the contrary is tendered by a party.

Whether the issue of whether a witness may give sworn evidence is raised by the court or by one of the parties, s.55 provides that the party who desires the witness to be sworn bears the burden of proving on the balance of probabilities that the witness is aged 14 or more and that he sufficiently appreciates the above-mentioned matters. Section 55 also provides that proceedings to determine the competence of a witness will take place in the absence of the jury, that expert evidence may be received for the purpose of determining whether a witness may be sworn and that any questioning of the witness for this purpose will be conducted by the judge.

Where a person is competent to give evidence in criminal proceedings but may not give sworn evidence due to the operation of s.55 of the 1999 Act, s.56 of the 1999 Act provides that the witness will give unsworn evidence.

CIVIL PROCEEDINGS

Limited mental ability and communication difficulties

A person called to give evidence in civil proceedings who, in the opinion of the judge, does not sufficiently appreciate the seriousness of the occasion or does not realise that giving evidence under oath involves more than the everyday duty of telling the truth is not competent (*R. v Bellamy* (1986)). In determining the competence of a witness, the judge may examine the witness and hear expert psychological evidence (*R. v Deakin* (1994); *R. v Hampshire* (1995)). Indeed, if the witness is mentally ill, it may be that the judge, having heard the evidence of the expert, can deal with the issue of competence without the necessity of examining the witness (*R. v Barratt* (1996)). If the witness's incapacity is only short term, *e.g.* when it is caused by drink or drugs, the judge may be prepared to adjourn (*R. v Baines* (1987)).

A person incapable of communicating his evidence to the court, *e.g.* because the person is deaf and dumb and is incapable of communicating by sign language through an interpreter, is also incompetent (*R. v Whitehead* (1866)).

Children

In civil proceedings a child (a person under the age of 18— Children Act 1989, s.105) may be competent to give sworn testimony. This will be the case if, in the opinion of the judge, the child sufficiently appreciates the seriousness of the occasion and realises that giving evidence under oath involves more than the everyday duty of telling the truth (*R. v Hayes* (1977) and *R. v Campbell* (1983)). Secondly, if a child is not competent to give sworn testimony in civil proceedings, the child may give unsworn testimony if, in the opinion of the judge, the child both understands that he is under a duty to speak the truth and has sufficient understanding to justify the reception of his evidence (Children Act 1989, s.96). Finally, if a child is neither competent to give sworn testimony nor competent to give unsworn testimony in civil proceedings then the child is incompetent and its evidence may not be received.

3. CORROBORATION AND SUPPORTING EVIDENCE, IDENTIFICATION EVIDENCE AND LIES TOLD BY THE ACCUSED

CORROBORATION AND SUPPORTING EVIDENCE

What is corroboration?

Essentially, one item of evidence is corroborated by another when the reliability of the former is confirmed by the latter. In English Law, however, in order for one piece of admissible evidence to be capable of corroborating another, the former piece of evidence must, as was recognised by the Court of Criminal Appeal in R. *v Baskerville* (1916), satisfy two fundamental requirements:

(1) The corroborative evidence must be independent of the witness whose evidence requires corroboration.

(2) The corroborative evidence must connect the accused with the commission of the crime by confirming in a material particular both that the crime was committed and that it was committed by the accused.

Corroboration is now rarely required by English Law

In English Law, corroboration is only required in those exceptional situations in which statute has imposed a corroboration requirement. For example, a person cannot be convicted of speeding if the only evidence that he was speeding is the uncorroborated evidence of a single witness (Road Traffic Regulation Act 1984, s.89). Thus, D cannot be convicted of speeding solely upon the evidence of W, who is prepared to testify that he saw D exceeding the speed limit, but D may be convicted if W's evidence is confirmed by X, who was with W when D's car passed them, or if W's evidence is confirmed by some mechanical means (*e.g.* by the speedometer of W's car or by a speed gun) (*Nicholas v Penny* (1950)). Corroboration requirements are also imposed by statute in the contexts of perjury and treason by, respectively, s.13 of the Perjury Act 1911 and s.1 of the Treason Act 1795. Corroboration warnings were formerly required in a number of situations.

The common law does not require the corroboration of a witness's evidence though, prior to statutory reform in the late

1980s and 1990s (see below), a trial judge was formerly required to warn the jury of the danger of convicting upon the uncorroborated evidence of three classes of witness. The relevant classes of witness were children, accomplices of the accused who were giving evidence for the prosecution and sexual offence complainants. The judge was required to explain to the jury why it was dangerous to convict upon the uncorroborated evidence of the relevant witness, to explain what was meant by corroboration and to identify for the jury evidence capable in law of providing corroboration. It was for the jury to decide whether the potentially corroborative evidence identified by the judge did, in fact, corroborate the evidence of the relevant witness. Moreover, even if the jury rejected the potentially corroborative evidence or if there was no evidence capable in law of providing corroboration, the jury were still entitled to convict solely upon the evidence of the relevant witness if they accepted it. Further, the courts also recognised that where an unreliable witness did not fall within one of these three classes it might still be necessary for the trial judge to give the jury an appropriate warning (for example: in consequence of the mental state and criminal connection of the witness (*R. v Spencer* (1987); *R. v Smails* (1987)); where the witness was a co-accused giving evidence in his defence against the accused (*R. v Cheema* (1994)); or, if the witness may have had an improper purpose of his own to serve when giving evidence against the accused (*R. v Beck* (1982))).

Following statutory reform, when should a judge now warn the jury of the dangers of relying on a witness's evidence and what form should the warning take?

Statutory reform has abolished the requirement that the judge give the jury a corroboration warning in respect of the evidence of witnesses falling within one or more of the three classes of witness referred to above, rendering the concept of corroboration in its technical legal sense of extremely limited significance in criminal proceedings.

First, s.34(2) of the Criminal Justice Act 1988 (as amended by the Criminal Justice and Public Order Act 1994) removed the requirement that the judge give a warning in respect of convicting upon the uncorroborated evidence of a child. Once this provision came into force, the only remaining classes of witness in respect of whose evidence a corroboration warning was required were the accomplice who gave evidence for the prosecution and the sexual offence complainant (*R. v Pryce* (1991)). Secondly, s.32(1) of the Criminal Justice and Public Order Act 1994 removed the requirements that the judge give a warning in respect of convicting upon the uncorroborated evidence of an accomplice who gave evidence for the prosecution or that of a sexual offence complainant.

The extent to which a trial judge should now give some form of warning following the abolition of these final two warning requirements was considered by the Court of Appeal in *R. v Makanjuola* (1995). So far as the need to warn the jury is concerned, their Lordships made clear that whilst the judge possesses discretion to give a warning, he will not be required to do so simply because the witness is an accomplice of the accused who is testifying for the prosecution or is a sexual offence complainant. Rather, a warning is appropriate where there is an evidential basis for suggesting that a witness's evidence is unreliable. This may, for example, be revealed by the content and quality of the witness's evidence or by evidence revealing that the witness has a grudge against the accused or that the witness has made false sexual offence complaints in the past.

So far as the nature of the warning is concerned, their Lordships made clear that a formal corroboration warning is no longer required. Thus, it is no longer necessary to explain to the jury what is meant by evidence capable of providing corroboration. Rather, when a trial judge in the exercise of his discretion decides that a warning is required, the warning should form part of his review of and comments upon the evidence, and the nature of the warning is for the judge to determine. Thus, it might be sufficient simply to urge the jury to be cautious when considering placing reliance upon the evidence of the relevant witness. Alternatively, the judge may feel that it is necessary to advise the jury to look for evidence supporting that of the relevant witness before placing reliance upon it. It appears, however, that evidence which is not independent of the witness whose evidence requires support is not capable of amounting to supporting evidence (*R. v Islam* (1998)). Thus, if C tells W that she was indecently assaulted by D and C then testifies to this effect, W's repetition in court of C's statement to W is not independent evidence and thus is not capable of amounting to supporting evidence.

Finally, as was indicated above, the courts formerly recognised that where a corroboration warning was not required in relation to the evidence of a witness, an appropriate warning might still be required in consequence of the witness's mental state and criminal connection or where the witness was a co-accused giving evidence in his defence against the accused or where the witness had an improper purpose of his own to serve. Following the abolition of the corroboration warning requirements it was held by the Court of Appeal that the approach laid down by the Court of Appeal in *R. v Makanjuola* should also be applied in relation to the evidence of such witnesses (*R. v Muncaster* (1999)). There is, however, more recent authority for the proposition that an appropriate warning should still routinely be given where a co-accused gives evidence against the accused (see, for example, *R. v Francom* (2000) and *R. v Jones* (2004)).

IDENTIFICATION EVIDENCE

What are the "Turnbull guidelines?"

The Court of Appeal in *R. v Turnbull* (1977) laid down guidelines which are applicable when the prosecution's case against the accused is wholly or substantially based upon disputed identification evidence. Essentially, the trial judge should warn the jury to be cautious when considering placing reliance upon the evidence of one or more witnesses who have identified the accused, explaining to them that such witnesses may be both convincing and mistaken. The judge should direct the jury to consider the circumstances in which an observation was made. Thus, they should be directed to consider factors such as: the duration of the period of observation; the distance between the witness and the person observed; the quality of the light; whether the observation was impeded in any way; whether the witness knew the accused and, if so, how many times they had met or how memorable their meetings had been; the length of time between the observation and the witness identifying the accused to the police; and any material discrepancies between the witness's description to the police of the person observed and the actual appearance of the accused. Further, where the witness did know the accused at the time when the observation was made, the jury should be reminded that people do sometimes make mistakes in recognising friends and relatives.

Where identification evidence is of good quality (*e.g.* when the observation was made in good lighting by a friend of the accused who had a clear view of him a short distance away for several minutes) it is safe to leave the evidence to the jury provided that they have been given a warning in the terms outlined by the Court of Appeal (though no particular form of words is required). Where the quality of the identification evidence is poor, however (*e.g.* where the witness only had a fleeting glance of the person he observed or where the observation was made at a long distance and in bad light by a stranger), simply to warn the jury in the terms outlined by the Court of Appeal is not sufficient. Rather, in such circumstances, the judge should withdraw the case from the jury and direct them to acquit the accused unless there is other evidence which is capable of supporting the identification evidence. Where such evidence exists the judge should direct the jury's attention to it, but the judge should also direct them to ignore for this purpose any evidence which they might regard as providing support for an identification but which does not in fact do so. Examples of potentially supporting evidence are the evidence of other identification witnesses (though the jury should be warned that they all may be mistaken—see *R. v Weeder* (1980) and *R. v Breslin* (1984)) and, in certain circumstances, lies told by the accused (see below)).

If the court fails to comply with the *Turnbull* guidelines where they are applicable and the accused is convicted, the practical result (unless the identification evidence is of high quality) is likely to be that the accused's conviction will be quashed upon appeal.

Do the "Turnbull guidelines" apply to forms of identification other than identification of the accused by witnesses?

Where a witness identifies the accused from a photograph or video recording, the *Turnbull* guidelines are applicable (see, respectively, *R. v Blenkinsop* (1995) and *Taylor v Chief Constable of Cheshire* (1987)). Similarly, an appropriately modified version of the *Turnbull* guidelines is applicable in the context of voice identification by witnesses (*R. v Hersey* (1998)). Where, however, the jury themselves make an identification from a photograph or video recording without the assistance of a witness, it appears that the *Turnbull* guidelines are not applicable (*R. v Downey* (1995)). In such circumstances, however, the judge should, even so, direct the jury to consider factors such as the quality of the image and any change in the appearance of the accused between the time when the photograph or video recording was taken and the time of the trial (*R. v Dodson* (1984)).

Moreover, if there is strong evidence to the effect that the accused and another person were together at the time when the offence with which the accused is charged was committed and evidence identifying the other person is disputed, it appears that a *Turnbull* warning is required if the accused claims that he was not present (*R. v Bath* (1990)).

Further, it should be noted that where a witness identified not the accused but a car, whilst the *Turnbull* guidelines are not applicable, the jury should be directed to consider factors such as the opportunity which the witness had to identify the vehicle and the ability of the witness to distinguish between cars (*R. v Browning* (1991)).

Finally, where the issue before the court is not whether identification evidence was erroneous but, rather, is whether the identification witness was lying, a *Turnbull* warning is not required (*R. v Cape* (1996)).

Dock Identifications and breaches of Code D

A dock identification is one which is made in court by a witness who has not previously identified the accused at an identification parade or equivalent procedure. Normally, the court will exercise its exclusionary discretion (*i.e.* its discretion under s.78 of the Police and Criminal Evidence Act 1984) so as to prevent a dock identification from taking place (*R. v Fergus* (1993)).

The court, in the exercise of its exclusionary discretion (*i.e.* under s.78 of the Police and Criminal Evidence Act 1984) is likely to exclude identification evidence in the context of serious or deliberate breaches of Code D (which regulates the conduct of identification parades, etc) (*R. v Quinn* (1990)). Where the court admits identification evidence in the context of breaches of Code D (*i.e.* in the context of less serious breaches) an appropriate direction to the jury will be required (*R. v Forbes* (2001)).

THE ACCUSED'S LIES

A jury may be entitled to draw an inference of guilt from lies told by the accused either out of court or in court. It should be noted, however, that the jury should only draw such an inference if they are satisfied beyond reasonable doubt both that the accused did lie and that he lied because he was guilty and not for some other reason (see *R. v Burge* (1995); *R. v Pegg* (1995)). Thus, for example, if the jury believe that D, charged with rape, may have lied to the police about having had intercourse with V not because he raped her but because he did not want his wife to find out that he had had intercourse with her, then the jury should not draw an inference of guilt from D's lie.

A trial judge may be required to warn the jury as to the significance of the accused's lies, and, in particular, to warn them that they should only draw an inference of guilt from them if sure both that he lied and that he lied because he was guilty. It appears that the giving of such a warning (known as a "Lucas direction" (*R. v Lucas* (1981)) is usually necessary:

(i) Where an alibi is raised by the defence;

(ii) Where the judge advises the jury to look for evidence in support of the evidence of an unreliable witness (including evidence in support of poor quality identification evidence) and identifies lies which the accused has or may have told as potential supporting evidence;

(iii) Where the prosecution relies upon lies which the accused has or may have told as evidence of his guilt;

(iv) Where there is a danger that the jury may rely upon lies which the accused may have told as evidence of his guilt (*R. v Burge*; *R. v Pegg*).

The giving of a "Lucas direction" is not required where the alleged lie relates to a central issue of the case as, in such circumstances, the normal direction which the judge gives the jury concerning the burden and standard of proof will be adequate (*R. v Burge*; *R. v Pegg*). In general, a "Lucas direction" is not required in circumstances in which there is no danger that the jury may equate the fact that the accused has told a lie with his guilt (*R. v Middleton* (2001)).

4.   THE ACCUSED'S RIGHT OF SILENCE

THE COMMON LAW

Substantial inroads into the accused's common law right of silence were introduced by the Criminal Justice and Public Order Act 1994 (CJPOA) which permits the drawing of adverse inferences from the accused's silence in certain situations. The common law on silence is now only relevant in one situation, namely where an accusation is put to the accused by someone who is not in authority or charged with investigating crimes and the accused makes no reply. In such circumstances, the parties are said to be on "even terms" and the court may draw an adverse inference from the accused's silence on the basis that an innocent person would have uttered a denial (*R. v Parkes*(1976)). Section 34(5) of the CJPOA specifically preserves the drawing of inferences at common law in this situation.

DRAWING INFERENCES FROM SILENCE UNDER THE CRIMINAL JUSTICE AND PUBLIC ORDER ACT 1994

Section 34—Silence as to a fact later relied upon by the accused in his defence

Requirements for section 34 to apply:

1. The accused relies upon a fact in his defence which he did not mention when questioned under caution or charged.

    The accused relies upon a fact in his defence where he, or a defence witness, testifies as to the fact or even where it is revealed by a prosecution witness (*R. v Bowers* (1998)). Section 34 will not apply if the defence does not actually rely upon the relevant fact (*R. v Moshaid* (1998)) or if the prosecution fail to prove that the accused was aware of the relevant fact at the time of the alleged failure to mention it (*B (MT)* (2000)). Failure to mention a theory or speculation rather than a fact does not activate the section (*R. v Nickolson* (1999)), nor does failure in interview to make an admission which is later made at trial to a fact relied upon by the prosecution (*R. v Betts* (2001)).

2. The fact is one which the accused could reasonably have been expected to mention in the circumstances existing at the time.

All the relevant circumstances are taken into account in assessing what is reasonable. Thus, they can include, for example, the personal characteristics of the accused and any legal advice he received (*R. v Argent* (1987)), the complexity of the prosecution's case or how much of it has been disclosed to the accused (*R. v Roble* (1997)) and the nature of the questions put to him (*R. v Nickolson*).

[*Note:* no inference may be drawn under s.34 if the accused was at an authorised place of detention and was denied the opportunity to consult a solicitor when he failed to mention the relevant fact.]

What is the effect of section 34? Where s.34 applies, it allows the court both when determining whether there is a case to answer and in determining guilt to draw such inferences as appear proper from the failure to mention the relevant fact. The inference which may be drawn is either that the accused has fabricated the relevant fact since his police interview or that he had already begun to fabricate a defence when he was interviewed but was unwilling to mention it as he had not had the chance to think it through sufficiently to expose it to detailed questioning (*R. v Randall* (1998)).

Exclusionary discretion The trial judge retains a discretion to prevent the drawing of an inference under s.34 (s.38(6)). This may be exercised where, for example, the accused's silence follows an unlawful arrest or breach of PACE or the Codes of Practice (*R. v Pointer* (1997)) or the prejudicial effect of the evidence outweighs its probative value (*R. v Argent*).

Remaining silent on solicitor's advice The fact that the accused failed to mention a relevant fact because his solicitor advised him not to does not automatically render the failure reasonable, however good the advice in the circumstances (*R. v Condron* (1997)). What is relevant is not whether the advice was correct but whether it was reasonable for the accused to act upon it by remaining silent (*R. v Argent*). Where an accused genuinely acting on legal advice remains silent, inferences may still be drawn if the jury is satisfied that he had no explanation to give or none that would withstand questioning and investigation (*R. v Hoare* (2004)).

If the accused intends to rely upon the fact that he was advised by his solicitor to remain silent, he or his solicitor must reveal to the court the basis of the advice or the reasons for it (*R. v Condron*). This may lead to waiver of legal professional privilege. Waiver may also result if, during the course of a police interview, the accused, or his solicitor acting as his agent, give reasons for the accused's silence (*R. v Fitzgerald* (1998)).

Can the accused be convicted solely upon his silence as to a relevant fact? Such silence cannot form the sole or main basis of a conviction against him (s.38(3) and *Murray v UK* (1996)).

The trial judge's direction to the jury under section 34 The trial judge should direct the jury that they may not draw an inference unless they are satisfied both that the requirements of s.34 have been met and that the accused's silence can only sensibly be attributed to his having no answer to the charges against him or none which would withstand questioning and investigation (*R. v Betts*). (Thus, where the jury is satisfied that there is a plausible explanation for the accused's silence other than that he had no answer to the charge or none which would withstand inquiry, they may not draw an inference.) The trial judge should also remind the jury that an accused cannot be convicted solely or mainly upon an inference drawn under the section (*Murray v UK*). Failure to direct the jury correctly on all these matters may result in a violation of the right to a fair trial under Art.6 of the Convention (*Condron v UK* (2000)). Thus, in *R. v Betts*, a direction in terms which permitted the jury to draw an adverse inference even though they may have considered plausible the accused's explanation for his failure to mention a relevant fact, was a breach of Art.6.

Sections 36 and 37—Silence in response to a request to account for objects, substances, marks or one's presence at a particular place

Section 36 permits inferences to be drawn at trial from the accused's silence or failure to account for the presence of objects, substances or marks where the following conditions are satisfied:

1. The accused was under arrest.
2. An object, substance or mark was found at the place of the accused's arrest either in his possession, on his person, clothing or footwear.

3. The constable or Customs and Excise officer investigating the offence reasonably believed that the presence of the object, etc. might be due to the participation of the accused in the commission of the offence he specified.
4. The constable or Customs and Excise officer gave the accused the special caution, (see Code C, para.10.11), informed him of his belief and asked the accused to account for the presence of the object, etc.
5. The accused failed so to account.

Section 37 permits inferences to be drawn at trial from the accused's failure or refusal to account for his presence at the scene of the crime where the following conditions are satisfied:

1. The accused was under arrest.
2. He was found at a place, at or about the time the offence was alleged to have occurred.
3. The constable or Customs and Excise officer investigating the offence reasonably believed that the accused's presence at the scene at the time of his arrest might have been attributable to his participation in the offence.
4. The constable or Customs and Excise officer gave the accused the special caution (see Code C, para 10.11), informed him of his belief and asked the accused to account for the presence of the object.
5. The accused failed so to account.

[*Note:* (1) No inference may be drawn under s.36 or 37 if the accused was at an authorised place of detention and was denied the opportunity to consult a solicitor when he failed to account for the object, etc. or his presence at the particular place.

(2) The trial judge retains a discretion to prevent the drawing of an inference under s.36 or 37 (s.38(6)).]

Can the accused be convicted solely upon his silence or failure to account for the presence of objects etc. or his presence at a particular place? It is submitted that the position under s.34 (see above) also applies under ss.36 and 37, so that the accused cannot be convicted solely or mainly on an inference drawn under the section (*Murray v UK*).

The trial judge's direction to the jury under sections 36 and 37 Although the courts have yet to consider the appropriate direction under these sections, it is likely to be in terms similar to the direction under s.34.

Section 35—The drawing of inferences from the accused's silence at trial

Section 35 permits inferences to be drawn at trial, both from an accused's failure to testify at all and from the failure of an accused who has taken the stand to answer questions once there, provided the following conditions are satisfied:

1. The accused's guilt is in issue and his physical or mental condition is not such that it appears to the court undesirable for him to testify (a low IQ is not a mental condition which makes testifying "undesirable" (*R. v Friend* (1997))); and
2. Where the accused takes the stand but refuses to answer any questions, he must not have a "good cause" for his refusal.

This means that an inference may not be drawn from the accused's refusal to answer questions which he is not legally obliged to answer.

Exclusionary discretion The trial judge retains a discretion to prevent the drawing of an inference under s.35 (s.38(6)) but it ought only to be exercised if there is an evidential basis for doing so or in exceptional circumstances (*R. v Cowan* (1996)).

Can the accused be convicted solely upon his silence at trial? Such silence cannot form the sole or main basis of a conviction or even contribute to a prima facie case against him (s.38(3) and *Murray v UK*).

The trial judge's direction to the jury under section 35 In *R. v Cowan* and *Condron v UK*, the court held that when directing the jury the trial judge must draw their attention to the following matters:

1. The burden of proof remains on the prosecution and the standard of proof is beyond a reasonable doubt;
2. The accused possesses a right of silence;

3. An inference drawn from the accused's silence cannot on its own prove guilt and nor can a conviction be based mainly on silence;
4. The jury cannot draw an inference from silence unless they find that the prosecution has established a case to answer;
5. The jury may draw an adverse inference if they find that the accused's silence can only sensibly be attributed to his having no answer to the charges against him or none that would stand up to cross-examination, but they should not do so if they consider that there is another sensible explanation for his silence.

Failure to direct the jury correctly on these matters may result in a violation of the right to a fair trial under Art.6 of the Convention (*Condron v UK*).

---

5. EXAMINATION, CROSS-EXAMINATION AND RE-EXAMINATION OF WITNESSES

[*Note:* this chapter is written as though the evidence provisions of the Criminal Justice Act 2003 are already in force. The relevant provisions are due to be brought into force in 2005.]

This chapter deals with the three stages involved in questioning a witness in both civil and criminal trials:

— *Examination in chief*
— *Cross-examination*
— *Re-examination*

As with many topics in evidence, the issues of admissibility, effect and relevance are of primary importance and must be borne in mind whenever tackling a question on examination of witnesses.

EXAMINATION IN CHIEF

This is the first stage of the process of questioning a witness. Counsel for the party who has called the witness asks him questions in order to elicit from him evidence which is advantageous to that party's case.

The types of questions which may not be asked during examination in chief

The normal rules relating to the admissibility of evidence apply to examination in chief so that the party who has called the witness may not ask him to provide evidence which would be inadmissible at *any* stage of the trial, for example because it is hearsay evidence. In addition, there are rules particular to examination in chief which preclude the admission of certain other types of evidence. Thus, leading questions and, subject to exceptions, questions relating to a witness's previous consistent statements are *not* permitted during examination in chief.

Leading questions These are questions which either imply that a certain answer is expected from the witness (*e.g.* "Was the car which knocked you over a blue Rolls Royce?") or which presume certain disputed evidence has been accepted (*e.g.* "Did the defendant drive straight on after he had hit you?").

Such questions are admissible because it is not, in effect, the witness giving his own version of the events but rather counsel for the party who called him suggesting what he ought to say. Strictly speaking, preliminary questions about a witness's name and address are leading questions but these are permitted for expediency.

Questions concerning a witness's previous consistent or self serving statements Witnesses may frequently wish to bolster the credibility of their testimony by asserting that what they are now saying is consistent with oral or written statements they have made prior to trial, the hope being that the court is more likely to believe them if they have not wavered in their story. However, questions regarding such previous consistent or "self serving" statements are not permitted during examination in chief, (*R. v Roberts* (1942)). The rule also extends to prevent other witnesses testifying regarding the previous consistent statements. In addition to being inadmissible to show consistency, previous consistent statements are also inadmissible as evidence of the matter stated, being hearsay.

As with many evidential rules, the rule against previous consistent statements has exceptions and these are listed below.

Where such an exception applies, a witness may refer in chief to a previous consistent statement in order to show consistency, this being relevant to his credibility. The previous statement will, however, remain hearsay and, consequently, inadmissible as evidence of the matter stated unless an exception to the hearsay rule also applies.

Exceptions in criminal proceedings

[*Note:* Previous consistent statements admitted under all but the last of the following exceptions (wholly exculpatory statements) are admissible not merely as to credibility but also as evidence of the matter stated (CJA 2003, s.120).]

Recent complaint of a victim Section 120 (1), (4)–(7) & (8) of the CJA 2003 provide that, where the victim of an alleged offence testifies, and has previously made a complaint about the offence which is consistent with their testimony in court, their previous consistent statement (the complaint) is admissible.

If this exception is to apply, the following conditions must be met:

(a) The complaint must have been made as soon as could reasonably be expected after the alleged offence.
(b) The complaint was not made as a result of a threat or promise.
(c) The victim gives oral evidence in relation to the subject matter of the complaint before evidence of the complaint is adduced.
(d) Whilst testifying, the victim indicates that to the best of his belief he made the statement and that it is true.

Statements identifying or describing a person, place or object Section 120 (1), (4) & (5) of the CJA 2003 provide that, where a witness testifies and has previously made a statement identifying or describing a person, place or object which is consistent with their testimony in court, their previous consistent statement is admissible. As with recent complaints, the witness must indicate whilst testifying that to the best of his belief he made the statement and that it is true.

Statements used to memory refresh See below.

To rebut a suggestion during cross-examination that the witness has recently fabricated his testimony If opposing counsel makes a specific suggestion to a witness that he has recently made up the evidence which he is giving in court, and the witness has in fact already made a statement which is consistent with his present testimony, that previous statement may be admitted to rebut the allegation of recent fabrication (*Flanagan v Fahy* (1918)).

Wholly exculpatory statements made by an accused during interviews with the police which become admissible at trial (*R. v Pearce* (1979)).

Exceptions in civil proceedings

Statements made in civil proceedings which are adduced with the leave of the court Section 6(2)(a) of the Civil Evidence Act 1995 provides that a previous consistent statement is admissible in civil proceedings under s.1 of the Act as evidence of the matter stated provided the leave of the court is first obtained.

To rebut a suggestion during cross-examination that the witness has recently fabricated his testimony See above. The previous statement is admissible as of the matter stated without the leave of the court, see s.6(2)(b) of the Civil Evidence Act 1995.

What can be done if a witness cannot remember what he is supposed to say during examination in chief?

There are two possibilities depending upon whether the witness is experiencing problems remembering before he goes into court or whether he begins to experience difficulties once he has taken the stand.

Refreshing one's memory outside the witness box Before going into court, a witness may read through a documentary statement he has previously made in order to refresh his memory (*R. v Richardson* (1971)).

Refreshing one's memory in the witness box The position here differs depending upon whether the proceedings are civil or criminal.

Criminal proceedings Section 139 of the CJA 2003 provides that once a witness has begun to testify, he may refresh his memory from a document which he either prepared himself or which was prepared by another and verified (see below for meaning of term) by the witness at an earlier time provided the witness:

(a) Testifies that the document records his recollection of the matter at the time he made it; and
(b) His recollection of the matter is likely to have been significantly better at the time the document was made or verified than it is at the time he testifies.

Civil proceedings Once a witness has begun to testify he may, with leave, refresh his memory from a document which he either prepared himself or which was prepared by another and verified by the witness whilst the facts were still fresh in his memory (*R. v Mills* (1962)). (Verification merely involves the witness looking at the document and checking that what it states is correct or having the statement read out to him and then accepting that it is correct (*R. v Kelsey* (1982))). The trial judge may grant leave for the witness to refresh his memory from such a document:

(a) Where it was made contemporaneously with the events it described, *i.e.* at the time of the event or so soon after-wards that the facts were still fresh in the witness's memory (*R. v Richardson* (1971)); or
(b) If it was not made contemporaneously, in the exercise of his discretion (*R. v South Ribble Magistrate's Court Ex p. Cockrane* (1996)).

Admissibility of memory refreshing documents

Criminal proceedings Documents used to memory refresh are not normally admissible in criminal proceedings. However, the CJA 2003 provides two situations in which such a document will be admissible as evidence of the matter stated:

1. Under s.120(3), if a witness is later cross-examined on the memory refreshing document and it is received in evidence, the statement will be admissible provided the witness's oral evidence on the matter would itself have been admissible.
2. Under s.120(4) & (6), if:

(a) The witness gives oral evidence in the proceedings;
(b) The statement was made by him when the relevant matters were still fresh in his memory;
(c) He can no longer, and cannot reasonably be expected to, remember them sufficiently well to give oral evidence of them in the instant proceedings;
(d) He indicates whilst testifying that to the best of his belief he made the statement and that it is true; and
(e) His oral evidence on the matter would itself have been admissible.

Civil proceedings Memory refreshing documents are not normally admissible in civil proceedings except in the following circumstances:

1. The witness's evidence and the memory refreshing document are not consistent;
2. It is suggested during cross-examination that the document was fabricated (*R. v Sekhon* (1987));
3. The jury will have problems following the cross-examination of the witness without copies of their memory refreshing document to read (*R. v Sekhon*);
4. The party who called the witness wishes to admit the document and the witness is cross-examined on parts of it which the witness did not use for memory refreshing (*Senat v Senat* (1965)).

Such statements are admissible under s.1 of the Civil Evidence Act 1995 as evidence of the matter stated (ss.6(4) & (5)).

What can be done if one's witness fails to give the evidence he had been called to give, *i.e.* "fails to come up to proof"?

A witness who fails to come up to proof may either be treated by the court as merely unfavourable or as actually hostile to the party who called him, depending upon the reason for his failure. The distinction between these two types of witness is important as the action which the party who called the witness may take to remedy the situation depends upon how the witness is treated by the court.

Unfavourable witnesses A witness is unfavourable if it is clear to the court either that he does wish to provide favourable evidence but is, for some reason, *e.g.* memory loss, unable to do so or if his testimony is truthful but actually unhelpful to the party who has called him.

Action that may be taken If a witness proves to be unfavourable there is little that the party who called him can do other than to adduce further evidence to prove that which the witness has failed to prove, for example by calling other witnesses to counteract the evidence of the first (*Ewer v Ambrose* (1825)) in which a second witness was called to prove the existence of a partnership the first witness having failed to do so).

It is not permitted to discredit one's own witness by attacking his character and credit merely because he is unfavourable. Nor is it permitted to put to him a previous statement he has made which is inconsistent with his present testimony.

Hostile witnesses A witness is described as hostile if he clearly has no wish to tell the truth on behalf of the party who called him.

As a witness will not automatically be treated as hostile, the party who called him must first seek the judge's permission to have the witness declared hostile. The judge will take into account factors such as the witness's degree of co-operation and manner in assessing whether to declare him hostile. If the witness has made a previous inconsistent statement outside court, then, unless the witness is blatantly hostile, the judge and the party calling the witness ought to consider giving the witness the opportunity to refresh his memory from it. If the witness should refuse to do so and also to provide an explanation why his present testimony is inconsistent with his earlier statement, then the judge may consider that he should be declared hostile (*R. v Maw* (1994)).

Action that may be taken once a witness has been declared hostile

(1) Evidence may be adduced to contradict the witness.
(2) With the leave of the judge, the witness may be cross-examined and may be asked leading questions. He cannot, however, be treated in exactly the same way as any witness under cross-examination in that he cannot be discredited by being asked questions about his bad character or previous convictions.

(3) With the leave of the judge, the party who called the witness may prove that the witness has made a previous inconsistent statement. Before doing so, details of the occasion on which the statement was made must be given to the witness so that he may remember making the statement and he must then be asked whether he made such a statement (see s.3 of the Criminal Procedure Act 1865 which applies to both criminal and civil proceedings).

Relevance

In criminal proceedings, the witness's previous inconsistent statement is relevant both to the credit of the witness and also (provided the witness's oral evidence would be admissible) as evidence of the matter stated (CJA 2003, s.119). In civil proceedings, the previous statement is also relevant to both credit and as evidence of the matter stated (s.1 of the Civil Evidence Act 1995). The notice requirements provided by s.2 of the Act are unlikely to apply because it is not until the witness actually testifies in court that he or she may be declared hostile. Consequently, notice will not be considered "reasonable and practicable in the circumstances", see further Chapter 10.

What action may be taken if a hostile witness refuses to testify? Section 3 of the Criminal Procedure Act 1865 is inapplicable in this situation because the witness has not given any testimony with which his previous statement can be inconsistent. Thus, his previous statement may not be adduced under s.3. However, it may be adduced at common law with the leave of the judge. In *R. v Thompson* (1976), the Court of Appeal held that the judge has a common law discretion to permit cross-examination, including questions about a previous statement, of a hostile witness by the party who has called him.

Witnesses for whom special measures are required

Section 19 of The Youth Justice and Criminal Evidence Act 1999 (YJCEA 1999) permits a criminal court to give special measures directions aimed at improving the quality of evidence given in court by intimidated or vulnerable witnesses. Either side may request such a direction and the court may also itself raise the issue. A special measures direction will, however, only be given where the court is satisfied that the following conditions are met:

(a) The special measure(s) would be likely to improve the quality of the witness's evidence.
(b) The Home Secretary has notified the court that arrangements have been made for implementing the special measure in the area in which the court is located.
(c) The witness is an "eligible" witness.

How is "eligible witness" defined? An eligible witness is a witness other than the accused (ss.16, 17 and 33) who:

(a) Will be a child witness, *i.e.* under 17 years of age, at the time the court has to decide whether giving a special measures direction would be likely to improve the quality of the witness's evidence (ss.16 and 19). (Where the witness was a child witness at the date he or she made video recorded statements to the police to be used as examination in chief but has reached 17 years of age by the time the court has to determine whether to give a special measures direction, he is not an eligible witness but a "qualifying" witness); or
(b) In the opinion of the court, will give evidence the quality of which is likely to be reduced due to mental disorder, significant impairment of intelligence and social functioning or physical disability or disorder (s.16); or
(c) In the opinion of the court, will give evidence the quality of which is likely to be reduced due to the fear or distress of testifying. Where the witness is a sexual offence complainant, he or she is eligible under this provision as of right (s.17).

Which special measures should the court apply? Where the court is satisfied that a special measure would be likely to improve the quality of the witness's evidence, it should then determine which measure(s) in particular would be likely to maximise so far as practicable the quality of such evidence. The measures available to the court are: screening the witness so that he cannot see the accused; giving evidence by live TV link; giving evidence in private; the removal of wigs and gowns whilst the witness testifies; video recording of evidence; giving evidence via an intermediary and the use of devices to assist communication.

Special measures applicable to child witnesses and qualifying witnesses (s.21) In respect of such witnesses, the primary rule is that a video recording of the witness's evidence should be admitted as evidence in chief and his or her cross-examination and re-examination should be given by live TV link unless the court directs that they ought to be video recorded. However, video evidence should not be admitted if it is not in the interests of justice to do so or if its admission would not be likely to maximise the quality of the witness's evidence so far as is practicable.

The position differs where the child/qualifying witness is one in need of special protection, *i.e.* the proceedings involve one or more of the offences specified in s.35(3), namely certain sexual offences, kidnapping and any offence involving an assault on, or injury or threat of injury to any person. In respect of such witness's evidence, the primary rule will still apply even if compliance with it would not be likely to maximise the quality of the witness's evidence so far as is practicable. Further, where the proceedings involve one of the sexual offences listed in s.35(3), and the court directs that a video recording of the witness's evidence is admitted as evidence in chief, it should also direct, unless the witness objects, that cross-examination and re-examination are also video recorded.

CROSS-EXAMINATION

This is the second stage of the process of questioning a witness. It takes place after examination in chief and is the stage where a party may question his opponent's witness in an effort to gain favourable evidence or to undermine the witness's testimony. A party who fails to cross-examine a witness is taken to have accepted the witness's testimony and cannot later dispute it (*R. v Bircham* (1972)).

As with examination in chief, the normal rules relating to the admissibility of evidence apply to cross-examination. Unlike examination in chief, however, leading questions are usually allowed during cross-examination.

Witnesses must normally answer any questions which are put to them during cross-examination, even questions aimed at discrediting them (but see the effect of the CJA 2003, considered in Chapter 13).

Four rules relating specifically to cross-examination which are of particular importance for examination purposes are those relating to questions concerning collateral matters, cross-examination about a previous inconsistent statement, cross-examination by the accused in person, and cross-examination of a sexual offence complainant.

Questions concerning collateral matters

The rule The basic rule with regard to questions concerning collateral matters is that a witness may be asked questions about such matters only during cross-examination but, subject to the exceptions listed below, a witness's answer to such questions will be treated as final so that the cross-examining party may not call evidence in rebuttal (*R. v Edwards* (1991)).

What is a collateral matter? A collateral matter is one which is only relevant to the credit of the witness who is being cross-examined and to no other issue in the proceedings. Unfortunately, whether a matter is relevant to credit only is not always easy to determine. Thus, in *R. v Hitchcock* (1847), the court proposed a test to determine whether a matter is collateral. The test is basically as follows. If the party who is cross-examining the witness could not have called evidence on the matter if the witness had not been called, because the matter is not relevant to an issue in the proceedings, the matter is collateral only and the witness's answer will be treated as final. If, on the other hand, the cross-examining party could have called evidence on the matter whether or not the witness had been called, because the matter is relevant to an issue in the proceedings, the matter is not collateral and the witness's answer will not be treated as final.

An example of a case in which a matter was treated as collateral is *R. v Burke* (1858). A witness who had informed the court that he could not speak English was allowed to give his evidence through an interpreter. After he had done so, it was put to him in cross-examination that he had been heard speaking in English outside the court. This he denied and the court then had to determine whether his ability to speak English was a collateral matter, to which his answer would be treated as final. The court decided that, as the questioning related only to the witness's credit, it was collateral (the witness's knowledge of English not being an issue in the proceedings).

The exceptions to the rule regarding the finality of questions relating to collateral matters

(a) *Bias.* If a witness denies an allegation put to him during cross-examination that he is biased, although bias is a collateral matter, the cross-examination party may call evidence to prove the witness's bias. The following cases illustrate this exception.

In *R. v Mendy* (1976), the accused's husband was asked during cross-examination whether he had, prior to testifying, and in an attempt to adapt his evidence, spoken to someone who had heard the testimony of the prosecution witnesses. The husband denied this allegation. The Court of Appeal upheld the trial judge's decision to allow the prosecution to call evidence in rebuttal.

In *R. v Phillips* (1936), the accused was charged with incest. During cross-examination, his daughter (the alleged victim) and another daughter denied having been schooled by their mother into putting forward the allegation of incest. On appeal, the court held that the trial judge had been wrong in refusing to allow the defence to call evidence to rebut the daughters' denial.

In *R. v Busby* (1982), an allegation was put during cross-examination that police officers were prepared to cheat in order to obtain a conviction by fabricating evidence and threatening a defence witness. Although the court treated the questions as not being collateral but rather as relevant to an issue in the trial, the case has subsequently been interpreted (in *R. v Edwards,* below) as one falling within the bias exception so that the defence ought to have been allowed to call evidence to rebut the officers' denial.

A similar case to *Busby,* but one which fell outside the exception, is *R. v Edwards.* The accused argued in his defence that the evidence against him had been fabricated. Police officers who testified for the prosecution were cross-examined as to whether their testimony in earlier trials, which had resulted in acquittals or quashed convictions due to fabrication of the evidence, had been untrue. The Court of Appeal held that because the issue was of the police officers' credibility in the present proceedings, the cross-examination related to a collateral matter but did not involve a suggestion of bias and, therefore, the officers' answers ought to be treated as final.

(b) *Previous inconsistent statements.* Questions put during cross-examination concerning previous inconsistent statements are collateral. The witness's answers to such questions will not be final, though, and a previous inconsistent statement can be adduced in rebuttal, see below.

(c) *The previous convictions of a witness, other than the accused.* Section 6 of the Criminal Procedure Act 1865 has the effect that should a witness in either civil or criminal proceedings deny during cross-examination the existence of their previous convictions, cross-examining counsel may adduce evidence of those convictions in rebuttal (but this is subject to CJA 2003, s.100, see Chapter 13).

(d) *Witness's reputation for untruthfulness.* A witness may be called to state that the other side's witness is generally known to be untruthful (*R. v Longman* (1968)).

(e) *Disability of witness.* A medical witness may be called to attack a witness's credibility on the basis of their inability to give truthful testimony due to their physical or mental disability (*Toohey v Metropolitan Police Commissioner* (1965)).

Cross-examination about a previous inconsistent statement

Under ss.4 & 5 of the Criminal Procedure Act 1865 (applicable both in civil and criminal proceedings), a witness may be cross-examined about any previous inconsistent statement he has made. Before doing so, details of the occasion on which the statement was made must be given to the witness so that he may remember making the statement and he must then be asked whether he made such a statement. If he then denies making the statement, the cross-examining party may then prove that the witness did in fact make such a statement.

Relevance of a previous inconsistent statement

In **criminal proceedings**, the witness's previous inconsistent statement is relevant both to the credit of the witness and also (provided the witness's oral evidence would be admissible) as evidence of the matter stated (CJA 2003, s.119).

In **civil proceedings**, the witness's previous inconsistent statement is also relevant both to the credit of the witness and as evidence of the matter stated under s.1 of the Civil Evidence Act 1995 (s.6(5)).

Cross-examination by the accused in person

What restrictions are imposed on the right of an accused to cross-examine a witness in person? The YJCEA

1999 prevents the accused from personally cross-examining a sexual offence complainant (s.34) or a protected witness (s.35). A protected witness is one who is (a) either the complainant or someone who witnessed the commission of the offence and (b) under 17 years of age either at the date he or she gave evidence in chief or when his evidence in chief was video recorded. The trial judge also retains a discretionary power under s.36 to prevent the accused personally conducting the cross-examination of any other witness (except a co-accused). The discretionary power will only be exercised provided the court is satisfied:

(a) That the quality of the witness's evidence is likely to be adversely affected by the accused conducting the cross-examination and that it would be likely to be improved if he were prevented from doing so; and
(b) That such a ban would not be contrary to the interests of justice.

Who may conduct cross-examination of a witness where the accused is prevented from doing so in person? Where the accused is prevented from personally cross-examining a witness by virtue of ss.34, 35 or 36, the court must give the accused the opportunity to appoint a legal representative to conduct the cross-examination. If the accused chooses not to do so, the court must appoint a qualified legal representative to conduct the cross-examination of the witness if it considers it to be in the interests of justice to do so (s.38).

Is the judge required to direct the jury where he prevents the accused cross-examining a witness in person? Where the accused is prevented from personally cross-examining a witness by virtue of ss.34, 35 or 36, the judge may, if he considers it necessary, warn the jury:

(a) Not to draw inferences from this; or
(b) Where a qualified legal representative has been appointed by the court, to ensure that the accused is not prejudiced by the fact that it was not his own legal representative who undertook the cross-examination.

Cross-examination of a sexual offence complainant

Section 41 of the YJCEA 1999 provides that where the accused is tried for a sexual offence, no evidence may be adduced or question asked in cross-examination by or on behalf of the accused about any sexual behaviour of the complainant except with the leave of the court.

What does the term "sexual behaviour" mean? Sexual behaviour is defined in s.42 as being "any sexual behaviour or other sexual experience, whether or not involving the accused or other person, but excluding (except in s.41(3)(c)(i) and 5(a)) anything alleged to have taken place as part of the event which is the subject matter of the charge against the accused."

When may leave be granted? Sections 41(2) and 41(6) provide that the court may only grant leave for the evidence of sexual behaviour to be adduced or the complainant asked questions about it in cross-examination, where the following conditions are satisfied:

(i) The evidence or question relates to a specific instance (or instances) of the complainant's sexual behaviour.
(ii) The evidence or question falls within one of the five situations set out in s.41(3) and s.41(5).
(iii) Where the evidence or question falls within s.41(3), its purpose must not be to establish material to impugn the credibility of the complainant as a witness.
(iv) Refusal to grant leave might render unsafe a conclusion of the jury or court.

What are the five situations in which leave may be granted?

1. *The evidence or question goes no further than is necessary to rebut or explain prosecution evidence of the complainant's sexual behaviour* (s.41(5)). For the purposes of this condition, sexual behaviour includes behaviour which is alleged to have occurred as part of the offence.
2. *The evidence or question relates to a relevant issue in the case other than whether the complainant consented* (s.41(3)(a)). Section 41(3)(a) is wide enough to encompass the situation in which the accused's defence is that he honestly believed the complainant consented (*R. v A* (2001)).
3. *The evidence or question relates to a relevant issue of consent and the sexual behaviour to which the evidence or question relates is alleged to have taken place at or about the same time as the alleged offence occurred* (s.41(3)(b)). The term "at or

about the same time" is unlikely to extend beyond a 24 hour period before or after the offence (*R. v A*).

4. *The evidence or question relates to a relevant issue of consent and the sexual behaviour to which the evidence or question relates is so similar to the accused's version of the sexual behaviour of the complainant during the commission of the alleged offence that the similarity cannot reasonably be explained as coincidence* (s.41(3)(c)(i)). For the purposes of this condition, sexual behaviour includes behaviour which is alleged to have occurred as part of the alleged offence.

An example of the situation which this condition was intended to cover was given by Lord Steyn in *R. v A* as being where the complainant alleges rape; the accused's defence is that the complainant consented and then, following intercourse, tried to blackmail him by alleging rape; and the defence wish to ask the complainant whether on a previous occasion she had also tried to blackmail the accused.

5. *The evidence or question relates to a relevant issue of consent and the sexual behaviour to which the evidence or question relates is alleged to have been so similar to any other sexual behaviour of the complainant which occurred at or about the same time as the alleged offence that the similarity cannot reasonably be explained as coincidence* (s.41(3)(c)(ii)).

Section 41 was considered by the House of Lords in *R. v A* in which their Lordships held that the ordinary principles of statutory interpretation render s.41 incompatible with Art.6 as the section might require the court to exclude evidence relevant to the accused's defence, specifically, because it prevents an accused who has had a previous sexual relationship with the complainant from adducing evidence relevant to the defence of consent. Thus, their Lordships applied s.3 of the Human Rights Act 1998 which required them to read the section in a way which would be compatible with Art.6. Thus, they held that evidence and questions which are necessary to ensure the accused's right to a fair trial should not now be excluded under s.41(3)(c) even if the specified similarity is not established.

RE-EXAMINATION

This, the third and final stage of the examination of a witness, is the stage at which a witness who has been cross-examined may be re-examined by the party who called him. Re-examination is not essential but it does give the examining party an opportunity to ask about matters raised in cross-examination or, with the leave of the judge, any matters overlooked in examination in chief. As with examination in chief, leading questions may not be asked (*Ireland v Taylor* (1949)).

---

6. EVIDENCE OF OPINION

Primarily, witnesses are called to give evidence of facts which they have perceived and evidence of opinions which they have formed upon the basis of the relevant facts is not admissible, it being the role of the court, not that of the witnesses, to form such opinions. At times, however, the opinion evidence of a witness may be admissible because the opinion of that witness forms an issue before the court (*e.g.* the opinion of a person charged with handling stolen goods is admissible to prove that the accused believed the goods to be stolen *R. v Hulbert* (1979)). Moreover, for a variety of purposes, witnesses are permitted to give evidence of general reputation (for example, a character witness may give evidence of the general reputation of the accused in the neighbourhood where he lives (see *R. v Rowton* (1865) in Chapter 13 below)). The two major situations in which opinion evidence is commonly admitted, however, are, first, when a non-expert witness conveys facts which he has perceived to the court in terms of his opinion and, secondly, where an expert witness gives the court the benefit of his expert opinion in relation to a matter falling outside the experience of the court.

NON-EXPERT WITNESSES

In civil proceedings, where a non-expert witness conveys facts which he has personally perceived to the court in terms of his opinion, his statement of opinion is admissible as evidence of the facts which he perceived (Civil Evidence Act 1972, s.3(2)). It appears that the (common law) position in criminal cases is largely identical. Thus, in *R. v Davies* (1962), it was proper for a witness to state his opinion to the effect that when he and the accused met, "the accused was under the influence of drink". It should be noted, however, that a non-expert witness cannot state his opinion upon a matter the formation of a proper opinion in respect of which requires expertise (*R. v Loake* (1911)). Moreover, a confession in the form of a statement of opinion may be worthless if its maker does not possess sufficient knowledge or expertise to make his opinion of some value (*Bird v Adams* (1972)).

Is there any difference between the position of the non-expert witness in civil and in criminal proceedings? If there is a significant distinction between the position of the non-expert in civil and in criminal proceedings it is that in proceedings of the latter type the non-expert may not be permitted to state his opinion upon an ultimate issue (*i.e.* one which the court is required to determine). Thus, for example, in *R. v Davies*, in which the accused was charged with being unfit to drive through drink, the Court of Appeal held that a non-expert witness should not have been permitted to state that in his opinion the accused was "in no condition to handle a motor vehicle". In civil proceedings, the evidence of a non-expert witness upon an ultimate issue is admissible (Civil Evidence Act 1972, s.3(2)).

EXPERT WITNESSES

Essentially (and subject to the leave of the court being given where the party calling an expert fails to satisfy pre-trial disclosure requirements laid down by rules of court in criminal proceedings or subject to permission to adduce expert evidence being given under the Civil Procedure Rules 1998 in civil proceedings), the opinion evidence of an expert witness upon facts which have been proved by admissible evidence is admissible if it relates to a matter which falls outside the experience of the court.

When do rules of court require the disclosure of expert evidence in criminal proceedings? A party to criminal trial in the Crown Court who wishes to adduce expert evidence other than in relation to sentencing must either comply with pre-trial disclosure requirements laid down by the Crown Court (Advance Notice of Expert Evidence) Rules 1987 or obtain the leave of the court. Essentially, the rules require disclosure of a written statement of the expert's findings or opinions and also (but only where this is requested in writing by another party) both of the records of observations, tests, calculations or procedures which form the basis of such findings or opinions and of documents or things in respect of which such procedures were carried out. Where a party has reasonable grounds to believe that the disclosure of evidence under the 1987 Rules may lead either to the intimidation or attempted intimidation of one of that party's witnesses or, otherwise, to interference with the course of justice, however, then the party is not required to disclose the relevant evidence. Moreover, a party entitled to disclosure of a statement, record, etc. under the 1987 Rules may, in writing, waive his right to be furnished with it or may agree that the expert's findings and opinions will be furnished to him orally. The Magistrates' Courts (Advance Notice of Expert Evidence) Rules 1997, which apply in the context of summary trial, are of similar effect to the Crown Court Rules except that the duty of disclosure only arises where the accused pleads not guilty.

[*Note:* it appears that from April 2005 the relevant rules will be contained in the new Criminal Procedure Rules.]

The expert witness and Part 35 of the Civil Procedure Rules 1998 As is seen below, expert evidence is only admissible in relation to matters which fall outside the court's experience. In civil proceedings, however, under Part 35 of the Civil Procedure Rules 1998 (CPR), even where a matter does fall outside the court's experience, the court is empowered to exclude, restrict or limit the nature of expert evidence.

Under CPR, Part 35, the court's permission is required either to call an expert witness or to put an expert's report in evidence (CPR 35.4(1)), the court being required to restrict expert evidence to that which is reasonably required to resolve the proceedings (CPR 35.1). Even where the court gives a party permission to adduce expert evidence in civil proceedings, such evidence will be given by written report unless the court directs otherwise (CPR 35.5). In other words, a civil court will not normally permit an expert witness to be called to give oral evidence, expert evidence in civil proceedings normally taking the form of the expert's written report). Moreover, where the parties to civil proceedings wish to adduce expert evidence in relation to an issue, the court may direct that the expert evidence will be given by a single joint expert, who will be instructed by the parties jointly (CPR 35.7). In such circumstances, if the parties fail to agree a single joint expert, the court may select a single joint expert from a list which the parties have prepared or approved or may direct another method of selecting a single joint expert. Where the court does direct that expert evidence in relation to an issue be given by a single joint expert, the court may, in appropriate circumstances, subsequently permit one of the parties to instruct his own expert (*Daniels v Walker* (2000)).

CPR 35.3 provides that the expert is under a duty to help the court which overrides the expert's duty to the party who instructed him. In his report, the expert is required to state that he understands this duty, has complied with it and will continue to do so. The expert's evidence should be independent and unbiased and he should take all material facts into account, even those which detract from his opinion. If a matter falls outside his expertise or if he cannot reach a definite opinion, he should make this clear and if he changes his view after producing his report he should communicate this to the parties.

As required by CPR 35.10, an expert's report must, amongst other things, specify the expert's qualifications, the literature, etc. which the expert relied upon when making the report, and the expert's conclusions, it must set out the substance of the expert's instructions and must be verified by a "statement of truth". If a range of expert opinions exist in relation to the matter which the report concerns, the report must summarise these and must indicate why the expert formed his opinion. It must indicate which of the facts stated are within the expert's knowledge and must identify and state the qualifications of persons who carried out tests, experiments, etc. It must summarise the expert's conclusions and, if the expert's opinion is qualified, the nature of the qualification must be stated. If there are reasonable grounds to consider that the statement of instructions which the expert's report contains is inaccurate or incomplete, the court may order disclosure of documents or questioning of witnesses in relation to the instructions. If an expert's report does not comply with the requirements of CPR, Part 35 and/or the expert witness does not appear to have complied with his duty to the court, the court may, in appropriate circumstances, be prepared to exclude the expert's evidence in the exercise of its exclusionary discretion (*Stevens v Gullis* (1999)).

Under CPR, Part 35, where the court does not direct the use of a single joint expert, it will normally direct the parties to exchange expert reports simultaneously on a specified day. If a party fails to disclose an expert's report, the party will only be able to rely upon the report or call the expert with the court's permission (CPR 35.13). Once an expert's report has been disclosed, however, any party may use the report at the trial (CPR 35.11). Moreover, where an expert's report (including a single joint expert's report) is served on a party, the party is, within 28 days, entitled to put written questions about the report to the expert for the purpose of clarifying it (CPR 35.6). The expert's answers are treated as part of the report. If the expert does not provide answers, the court may direct that the party who instructed the expert cannot rely on his evidence.

CPR Part 35 empowers the court to direct a party to provide another party with information (*e.g.* concerning tests or experiments) which is accessible to the former but which is not reasonably accessible to the latter (CPR 35.9). Moreover, where the parties have their own experts, the court, in an attempt to identify and agree the expert issues, is empowered to direct discussions between the experts (CPR 35.12).

Finally, it should be noted that the Pre-Action Protocol for Personal Injury Claims and the Pre-Action Protocol for the Resolution of Clinical Disputes both make provision concerning the instruction of expert witnesses in civil proceedings. Essentially, the Personal Injuries Protocol (which primarily applies to fast track personal injury claims) encourages the parties to instruct a single joint expert. In contrast, the Clinical Disputes Protocol (which applies to medical negligence claims), whilst encouraging the parties to use experts economically and less adversarially, leaves it to them to decide whether to instruct a single joint expert.

Who is an expert? Only an expert is competent (or, in the words of s.3(1) of the Civil Evidence Act 1972 "qualified") to give expert evidence. It is for the judge, in criminal or in civil proceedings, to determine the competence of a witness to give expert evidence. Clearly, factors such as qualifications, training and experience will all be relevant but, fundamentally, if, by virtue of his experiences, the witness has acquired the necessary expertise, the fact that he lacks formal qualifications and training does not prevent him from being competent to give expert evidence (*R. v Stockwell* (1993)). Where a witness is not an expert, however, then, as was noted above, the witness cannot state his opinion upon a matter the formation of a proper opinion in respect of which requires expertise.

Must the expert have personally perceived the facts upon which his opinion is based?   Essentially, the facts upon which the opinion evidence of an expert is based must be proved by admissible evidence. Thus, it may be that the expert did himself perceive the relevant facts and can give evidence of them, in which case they may be proved by his evidence. Alternatively, where the expert did not himself perceive the relevant facts, it may be necessary to call another witness to prove them, the expert stating his opinion based upon the facts so proved. Thus, in *R. v Abadom* (1983), an expert witness was by his own testimony able to prove that the refractive indices of two samples of glass were the same because he had personally analysed the samples. In contrast, in *R. v Mason* (1911), an expert was only entitled to state his opinion as to whether wounds on a body which the expert had not examined were self-inflicted because a witness who had examined the body had been called to prove the relevant facts.

Where the expert did not personally perceive the facts upon which the opinion is based, it may, at times, be possible to prove those facts by relying upon hearsay evidence, though the weight of the hearsay evidence will, in general, be less than that of the evidence of a witness who personally perceived the relevant fact (the nature of hearsay evidence is considered in Chapter 9 below). As is seen in Chapters 9 and 12 below, under the hearsay provisions of the Criminal Justice Act 2003, hearsay evidence is only admissible in criminal proceedings where it falls within a statutory or preserved common law exception to the hearsay rule, where the court admits it under the inclusionary discretion conferred by s.114(1)(d) of the 2003 Act or by agreement of the parties. Conversely, hearsay evidence is now generally admissible in civil proceedings under s.1 of the Civil Evidence Act 1995 (see Chapter 10 below).

Section 127 of the Criminal Justice Act 2003 creates a new exception to the hearsay rule which relates to the evidence of expert witnesses. Under this new hearsay exception, an expert may base an opinion or an inference on a statement which was prepared for the purposes of criminal proceedings (or for those of a criminal investigation) by a person who had or may reasonably be supposed to have had personal knowledge of the matters stated if notice is given that the expert will base an opinion or an inference thereupon. Where an expert's evidence is based upon such a statement, the statement is treated as evidence of what it states. The court may, however, upon application by a party, order that it is not in the interests of justice for s.127 to apply. In deciding whether to so order, the matters the court should consider include the expense of calling the person who prepared the statement, whether the person could give relevant evidence that the expert could not give and whether the person can reasonably be expected to remember the matters stated well enough to give oral evidence thereof.

[*Note:* the expert's report is itself admissible in criminal proceedings under s.30 of the Criminal Justice Act 1988, but if the expert is not called to give oral evidence his report is only admissible under s.30 with the leave of the court.]

In forming his opinion, it may be that an expert does not merely consider the facts of the case with which he is concerned but also takes into account other information, such as that contained in specialist text books and articles. The expert may well have no personal knowledge of some or all of the information contained in these books or articles because, for example, they relate to scientific tests which he has not himself conducted or to phenomena which he has not personally perceived. Even so, the expert is entitled to take this information into account in forming his opinion (see *R. v Abadom*). In *R. v Abadom*, a scientist was required to determine whether broken glass found in the accused's shoe had come from a particular window. He determined and compared the refractive indices of the glass in the shoe and of glass from the window and found that they were the same. He also relied upon Home Office statistics which showed that only a small percentage of glass samples shared this refractive index. Thus, he concluded that there was strong evidence that the glass in the shoe had come from the window. The Court of Appeal held that the expert was entitled to rely upon the Home Office data.

[*Note:* the common law rule under which such evidence is admitted is preserved in criminal proceedings by s.118 of the Criminal Justice Act 2003.]

When does a matter fall outside the court's experience? Expert evidence is admissible (subject, in the context of civil proceedings, to the provisions of CPR, Part 35, considered above), where a court is required to determine an issue which falls outside its experience (*R. v Turner* (1975)). In other words, expert evidence is admissible where it is relevant to a matter on which the expert is qualified to give expert evidence (Civil Evidence Act 1972, s.3(1)). For example, if a jury is required to consider whether the accused could have killed the victim whilst the accused was sleepwalking, the jury is entitled to expert assistance, the capabilities of a sleepwalker being outside the experience of the average juror (*R. v Smith* (1979)). Equally, where a jury in reaching its verdict is required to take into account the characteristics of an accused who is said to be mentally ill or of sub-normal IQ, the evidence of psychiatrists or psychologists may be admissible (*R. v Maish* (1986)).

In contrast, expert evidence is not admissible in criminal or civil proceedings where the issue before the court is one which falls within the court's experience. Thus, for example, if a jury is required to consider whether it is likely that a normal person (*i.e.* one who is not mentally ill or of sub-normal IQ) would have been provoked in given circumstances, psychiatric advice is not required, and, consequently, is not admissible, the issue falling within the experience of the jury (*R. v Turner* (1975)). Equally, it has been held that a jury does not require expert advice in order to determine whether a publication is obscene (see *R. v Calder & Boyers* (1969)).

Fundamentally, whether a court requires the assistance of an expert will vary with the specific facts of the specific case before it. Thus, for example, whether a jury requires the assistance of a facial mapping expert in order to determine whether the man whose image was captured in a photograph is the man in the dock before them may depend upon factors such as whether the man in the photograph was wearing a disguise (*R. v Stockwell*). Similarly, a civil court may well require the assistance of an expert in the context of a claim arising out of a road traffic accident in order to draw inferences from matters such as skid marks and the nature of accident damage but may not require expert assistance in order to determine whether the defendant was driving too fast, should have seen the claimant or should have blown his vehicles' horn (*Liddell v Middleton* (1995)).

Whose opinion is decisive—the court's or the expert's?
Where expert evidence is admissible, the expert does not, or should not be permitted to, replace the tribunal of fact. Thus, for example, in a jury trial it should be the opinion of the jury, not the opinion of the expert, which determines the relevant issue. Equally, in a civil trial, it is the opinion of the judge, not that of

the expert witnesses, which determines the issues before the court. It is for the jury (or the judge in a civil trial) to determine what weight (*i.e.* probative value) should be given to an expert's evidence. Consequently, a jury should not normally be directed to accept the evidence of an expert (*R. v Lanfear* (1968)). Indeed, it will often be that the jury are required to choose between the opinions of two or more experts, prosecution and defence. Exceptionally, however, it may be that in the absence of other evidence a jury should be directed to accept "unequivocal, uncontradicted" expert evidence (*R. v Sanders* (1991)). Certainly, a direction to a jury encouraging them to undervalue the evidence of an expert is equally improper (see *R. v Anderson* (1972)). Similarly, whilst, in civil proceedings, the judge is not inherently required to accept even the opinion of a single joint expert (*Fuller v Strum* (2001)), there may be circumstances in which the judge will effectively be required to accept cogent expert evidence which is uncontradicted. Whilst it is for the tribunal of fact and not for the expert to determine the issues before the court, this does not prevent the expert from stating his opinion upon an ultimate issue (*i.e.* the very issue the court is required to determine) provided that expert assistance is required. That this is so in civil proceedings is made clear by s.3(3) of the Civil Evidence Act 1972 (*Re M & R (Minors)* (1996)). So far as criminal proceedings are concerned, the common law "ultimate issue rule" has not been abolished by statute and thus, technically, an expert witness should not give his opinion on an ultimate issue in criminal proceedings. In practice, it appears that experts are often permitted to give such evidence in criminal proceedings, though the jury must be reminded that it is for them, and not for the expert, to determine the relevant issue (*R. v Stockwell*), and the criminal courts do still appear to apply the ultimate issue rule in some contexts, such as that of DNA evidence (*R. v Doheny* (1997)).

---

7. PRIVILEGE AND PUBLIC INTEREST IMMUNITY

In this chapter we will consider the nature of three forms of privilege, namely, the privilege which attaches to communications made "without prejudice", the privilege against self-incrimination and legal professional privilege. We will also consider the nature of public interest immunity. Essentially, where a party is entitled to claim privilege and does so, he may be entitled to refuse to answer questions in court or to withhold inspection of documents and may also be entitled to require another person (*e.g.* his legal adviser or an expert witness) to do the same. A party entitled to claim privilege may, however, waive it (*i.e.* relinquish the right to claim it). Public interest immunity is not a form of privilege though, like privilege, a successful public interest immunity claim may entitle a party to refuse to disclose documents or answer questions.

COMMUNICATIONS MADE "WITHOUT PREJUDICE"

When does the privilege arise?

Essentially, a communication is privileged as a "without prejudice communication" if made in the course of a genuine attempt to negotiate the settlement of a dispute (*Rush and Tompkins v GLC* (1989)). This will be so unless the communication is made upon an "open" basis. Thus, during a genuine attempt to negotiate a settlement, a party may make an admission of liability safe in the knowledge that, should the matter end up in court, the admission cannot be put in evidence against him without his consent. Whilst it is normal and correct practice to head a letter written in the course of such negotiations "without prejudice", and the presence or absence of such a heading will be taken into account by the court in determining whether the privilege arises (*Prudential Assurance Company Ltd v Prudential Assurance Company of America* (2003)), the presence or absence of such a heading is not decisive. Consequently, the fact that a letter is headed "without prejudice" does not, in itself, give rise to the privilege and, conversely, a letter written in the course of genuine negotiations aimed at settlement may be privileged even though the "without prejudice" heading is missing and even though it is headed "open letter" (*Dixon's Stores Group Ltd v Thames Television plc* (1993)).

Does the privilege come to an end when settlement is reached and can it be claimed against a third party?

The privilege subsists even after a settlement has been reached and not only prevents the party to whom the privileged communication was made from making use of admissions contained therein against its maker but also prevents third parties from so doing (*Rush & Tomkins v GLC*). Thus, where A makes an admission in the course of negotiations with B which are aimed at the settlement of a dispute between them, the communication is privileged whether or not a settlement was eventually reached and, consequently, neither B nor C (a third party) can make use of the admission in litigation concerning its subject-matter. The parties to "without prejudice negotiations" may, however, jointly waive the privilege. Moreover, it appears that, in the context of litigation by a third party against one of the parties to the negotiations, the privilege may be waived by that party alone (*Muller v Linsley & Mortimer (a Firm)* (1994)).

Does the privilege only apply to admissions?

As between the parties to the negotiations, the privilege applies to all communications between the parties, not merely to admissions (*Unilever plc v Proctor and Gamble* (1999)). As between a party to the negotiations and a third party, however, the privilege only applies to admissions (*Murrell v Healy* (2001)).

Exceptions and extension

The operation of the privilege is subject to a number of exceptions. For example, it does not prevent the admission of communications where the issue before the court is whether a settlement was reached (*Walker v Wilsher* (1889)). Conversely, it should be noted that the ambit of the privilege has been extended, in the context of matrimonial conciliation, to encompass mediation between parties by a mediator, such as a marriage guidance counsellor (see, for example, *Mole v Mole* (1951)).

SELF-INCRIMINATION

When does the privilege arise?

Basically, a person is not required to answer a question in court, and is entitled to withhold inspection of a document sought by another party, if answering the question or permitting inspection of the document would tend to expose him to a criminal charge which is reasonably likely to be preferred or to proceed ings in respect of a penalty or forfeiture which are reasonably likely to be brought (*Blunt v Park Lane Hotel Ltd* (1942)). A person entitled to claim the privilege may, however, waive the right to do so.

[*Note:* an example of a penalty is one imposed by the Inland Revenue; an example of forfeiture is forfeiture of property under a lease.]

Statutory removal of the privilege

The right to claim the privilege against self-incrimination has been removed by statute in a variety of contexts, both expressly and by necessary implication. Thus, for example: where the accused chooses to testify in criminal proceedings, statute expressly provides that he may be asked questions tending to criminate him (Criminal Evidence Act 1898, s.1(e)).

Similarly, statute expressly provides that a person may be asked questions which may incriminate that person or his or her spouse or may be required to comply with an order of the court which is of the like effect in proceedings for the recovery or administration of property, for the execution of a trust or for an account of property or dealings therewith (Theft Act 1968, s.31). Where a person answers such a question or complies with such an order as required by s.31, however, the statements or admissions which the person makes are not admissible in evidence against the person or the spouse in subsequent proceedings for an offence under the Theft Act 1968 unless, in the case of the spouse, the marriage took place after the statements or admissions were made.

An example of the implied removal of the privilege by statute is provided by the examination of persons by inspectors appointed by the Department of Trade and Industry under the authority of the Companies Act 1985. Whilst the relevant statutory provisions do not expressly remove the privilege, if the privilege could be claimed by persons so examined this would prevent the attainment of the relevant statutory purpose (namely, the investigation of fraud *Re London United Investments plc* (1992)).

Human Rights

Where statute expressly or impliedly removes the privilege against self-incrimination and does not provide an alternative protection, thus compelling a person, upon pain of a possible fine or imprisonment, to provide evidence which is later used in subsequent criminal proceedings against him, this is likely to result in a violation of Art.6 of the European Convention on Human Rights (*Saunders v UK* (1996)). A number of statutory provisions, which removed the privilege against self-incrimination and did not prevent the use of evidence obtained by compulsion from being used in subsequent criminal proceedings against the person from whom the evidence was obtained, were amended by the Youth Justice and Criminal Evidence Act 1999 in order to avoid future violations of Art.6. An example is provided by the provisions concerning examination of persons by Department of Trade and Industry inspectors which were referred to above. The effect of the amendments to these provisions is, essentially, that, in subsequent criminal proceedings, the prosecution cannot adduce evidence concerning the accused's answers to the inspectors' questions and cannot ask questions concerning those answers.

It should be noted, that the relevant amendments do not prevent the use in evidence of pre-existing documents or other pre-existing evidence which the accused was compelled to produce. This is so because the Art.6 right not to incriminate oneself (unlike the English Law privilege against self-incrimination, when it has not been removed by statute) does not encompass such evidence (*Saunders v UK*).

Judicial alternatives to the privilege

A civil court may be prepared to order a person to disclose information, the production of which might ordinarily expose him to a criminal charge, in circumstances in which the court is able to ensure that the production of the relevant information will not be used against that person in subsequent criminal proceedings. Thus, for example, disclosure has properly been ordered subject to a condition that the information disclosed would not be used in criminal proceedings against the person required to disclose the relevant information. It appears, however, that such an order should only be made where the prosecuting authority agrees not to use the information so disclosed in criminal proceedings against the person required to disclose it (*A.T. & T. Istel v Tully* (1993)).

When will a judge uphold a claim of privilege?

As was indicated above, the privilege against self-incrimination arises if answering a question or permitting inspection of a document would tend to expose the party entitled to claim the privilege to a criminal charge which is reasonably likely to be preferred or to proceedings in respect of a penalty or forfeiture which are reasonably likely to be brought In determining whether the privilege against self-incrimination arises, the judge must consider not merely whether the answer to a question or the production of a document would directly criminate the person answering the question or producing the document but also whether it would provide evidence which, in combination with other evidence, might form the basis of a charge against that person (*R. v Slaney* (1832); *R. v Boyes* (1861)). Moreover, even if answering a question or producing a document would either incriminate the person answering the question or producing the document or provide evidence against that person, the judge will not uphold a claim of privilege if the possibility that a charge will be preferred is a remote one such as would not influence the conduct of a reasonable man (*R. v Boyes*). Further, it appears that where the person claiming privilege is already exposed to the risk that criminal charges will be preferred and that answering a question or producing a document will not increase that risk, the claim will not be upheld (*R. v Khan* (1982)).

Where the privilege has not been removed by statute, is its application in civil and in criminal proceedings identical?

A person can no longer claim the privilege against self-incrimination in civil proceedings upon the basis that answering a question or producing a document would tend to expose that person to a forfeiture (Civil Evidence Act 1968, s.16(1)(a)). Moreover, in civil proceedings, a spouse may refuse to answer a question or to produce a document if answering the question or producing the document would tend to expose his or her spouse to a charge or penalty (Civil Evidence Act 1968, s.14(1)(b)). Further, in civil proceedings a person cannot claim the privilege merely because answering a question or producing a document would expose that person to a charge or penalty under the law of a foreign country (Civil Evidence Act 1968, s.14(1)(a)).

Whether, within the context of criminal proceedings, a spouse can claim the privilege so as to prevent the incrimination of his or her spouse and whether, within that context, exposure to a criminal charge or a penalty under foreign law can give rise to the privilege has not been conclusively determined. It should be noted, however, that, in any event, a penalty imposed under the law of the European Community is imposed under domestic law, not under foreign law (*Rio Tinto Zinc Corporation v Westinghouse Electric Corporation* (1978)).

LEGAL PROFESSIONAL PRIVILEGE

When does the privilege arise?

Basically, a client is entitled to refuse to answer questions in court or to withhold inspection of documents sought by another party, and is also entitled to require his legal adviser to do the same, where the questions concern or the documents comprise confidential communications between the client and the legal adviser which were made for the purposes of obtaining or giving legal advice. Further, the privilege also extends to encompass questions or documents concerning or comprising confidential communications between the client or his legal adviser and third parties (*i.e.* witnesses) if the dominant purpose of the relevant communications was that of preparing for litigation which has commenced or is contemplated. In this latter case the client is also entitled to require the third party to refuse to answer the relevant question or produce the relevant document. The former of these two forms of legal professional privilege is commonly referred to as "legal advice privilege", the latter commonly being referred to as "litigation privilege".

Must a lawyer-client relationship exist in order for the privilege to arise?

If a lawyer-client relationship does not exist, then the privilege will not arise. Thus, for example, if C asks L, his friend, for his confidential advice in respect of a legal matter, the advice given by L will not be privileged, even though L is a lawyer, if L does not give it in the course of performing his professional duties (*Smith v Daniel* (1875)).

Are all lawyer-client communications or communications between opposing parties confidential?

Not all lawyer-client communications are confidential. For example, if a client retains a solicitor and informs the solicitor of his address for correspondence purposes, it appears that, in the normal course of events, the solicitor's knowledge of the client's address does not amount to a professional confidence (*Ex p. Campbell* (1870)). Moreover, it should be noted that communications between opposing parties to legal proceedings are not confidential (*Parry v News Group Newspapers* (1990)) though, as was seen above, they may be still be privileged if they amount to "without prejudice communications".

In order for the privilege to arise, is it necessary that litigation has commenced or is contemplated?

So far as confidential communications between lawyer and client are concerned, all that is necessary is that the purpose of the communications was that of obtaining or giving legal advice. Therefore, in order for the form of legal professional privilege referred to as "legal advice privilege" to arise, it is not necessary that litigation had commenced or was contemplated at the time when the communication was made. Thus, for example, legal advice privilege may arise in the context of communications between solicitor and client concerning the drafting of a lease by the solicitor for the client may be privileged even though litigation had not arisen and was not contemplated at the relevant time (*Balabel v Air India* (1988)). In order for legal advice privilege to arise, however, it appears that the advice which is sought or given must take place in a "relevant legal context" (and, thus, some forms of business advice which a solicitor gives to his client may not be privileged) (*Three Rivers DC v Governor and Company of the Bank of England* (2004)).

As regards communications with third parties (*i.e.* expert witnesses or witnesses of fact), such communications are only privileged by legal professional privilege in the form of "litigation privilege" if the dominant purpose of the communications was that of preparing for litigation which has commenced or is contemplated. In *Waugh v British Railways Board* (1980) the relevant communication was a report concerning the details of a railway accident which had been prepared equally for the purpose of accident prevention and for the purpose of providing the Board's legal adviser with information which he required in the context of contemplated litigation. Since informing the Board's legal adviser was not the dominant purpose of the two, the House of Lords held that the report was not privileged.

Finally, it should be noted that litigation privilege will not arise where a communication was made for the purposes of non-adversarial proceedings (*Three Rivers DC v Governor and Company of the Bank of England (No.5)* (2003)).

Can the privilege attach to pre-existing documents which the client subsequently sends to the lawyer or to the third party?

Where a document was not privileged at the time when it was created, the fact that it is subsequently sent by the client to a lawyer or to an expert witness does not entitle the client to subsequently claim that it is privileged. Thus, if a client sends an invoice containing a sample of his handwriting to his solicitor and the solicitor sends the invoice to a handwriting expert, the client is not entitled to claim privilege in respect of the invoice (*R. v King* (1983)).

Where, for the purposes of litigation which has commenced or is contemplated, a lawyer makes a copy of an unprivileged document which has never been in the clients hands, the copy may be privileged (*Watson v Cammell Laird* (1959); *Dubai Bank v Galadari* (1989)). Equally, copies of unprivileged document in the lawyer's hand may be privileged if the lawyer used his skill to compile the collection of documents, inspecting the documents might reveal the nature of his advice to his client and the documents are not the client's own documents (*Lyell v* Kennedy (1884); *Sumitomo Corp v Credit Lyonnais* (2002)).

Does the operation of the privilege prevent a witness of fact from giving evidence of facts which he has personally perceived?

Where a third party (*i.e.* an expert witness or a witness of fact) has perceived relevant facts, the fact that he has engaged in privileged communications with the lawyer or the client does not prevent him from being called as a witness by another party to the relevant legal proceedings. If the client asserts his privilege, the witness cannot give evidence as to the content of the privileged communications, but the existence of the privilege does not prevent the third party from giving evidence of the facts which he has perceived (*Harmony Shipping Co v Saudi Europe* (1979)).

Where two clients jointly retain a common legal adviser, can one successfully claim privilege against the other in respect of communications between the clients and the legal adviser?

Where two clients jointly retain a legal adviser, either may claim that communications made to the lawyer in the capacity of their joint legal adviser are privileged as against third parties but neither may claim that such communications are privileged as against each other (*Re Konigsberg* (1989)).

Can the client successfully claim privilege against another party who shares a joint interest with him in the subject-matter of the privileged communication or with whom he has a common interest in the outcome of litigation?

A client cannot successfully claim privilege against a person with whom the client shares a joint interest in the subject-matter of the privileged communication. Thus, for example, trustees cannot maintain privilege against a beneficiary in respect of communications concerning a disposition of trust property (*In Re Postlethwaite* (1887)). They could, however, maintain privilege in such communications against third parties. The same may be true where parties with a common interest in litigation retain a common legal adviser and exchange information (*Buttes Gas and Oil Co v Hammer (No.3)* (1981)).

Can the right to claim legal professional privilege be waived?

Legal professional privilege can only be claimed or waived by the client or on behalf of the client (*Proctor v Smiles* (1886)). If the client chooses to claim privilege it cannot be waived on their behalf by the legal adviser or the third party. Equally, where the client chooses to waive privilege, it cannot be claimed on their behalf by the legal adviser or the third party. It should be noted, however, that the legal adviser, whilst acting in the capacity of the client's agent, may possess the authority to waive privilege on the client's behalf. Thus, if a solicitor, whilst acting on his client's behalf, mistakenly permits another party to inspect a privileged document, this may amount to a waiver of privilege (*Guiness Peat Properties Ltd v Fitzroy Robinson Partnership* (1987)). Equally, if a client's barrister mistakenly reads out part of a privileged document in court, this, too, may amount to a waiver of privilege in the entire document (*Great Atlantic Insurance v Home Insurance* (1981)). Moreover, where, in the course of legal proceedings, privilege is waived by one party in a communication which concerns a particular transaction, this may result in the other party being entitled to disclosure of other communications concerning the same transaction (*General Accident Fire and Life Assurance Corporation Ltd v Tanter* (1984)). Similarly, where a former client sues his former solicitor in negligence, this may give rise to an implied waiver of privilege by the client in relation to lawyer-client communications concerning the transaction which forms the subject matter of the negligence proceedings (*Lillicrap v Nalder* (1993)).

Where a party has obtained possession of copies of privileged documents can he use these as secondary evidence to prove the contents of the originals?

Essentially, where a party to legal proceedings obtains possession of copies of privileged documents, the party may use the copies as secondary evidence to prove the contents of the originals (*Calcraft v Guest* (1898)). It may be, however, that, before the secondary evidence is adduced, a court will be prepared to grant the party entitled to claim privilege an injunction preventing the party in possession of the copies from making use of them (*Lord Ashburton v Pape* (1913)).

Basically, it appears that a court will be prepared to grant an injunction preventing the use of secondary evidence to prove the contents of a privileged document if the party entitled to claim the privilege applies for the injunction before the copies have been adduced in evidence and provided that there is no reason why the court, in the exercise of its discretion, should refuse to grant an equitable remedy (*Goddard v Nationwide Building Society* (1987)). In general, such an injunction will be granted even though the conduct of the party wishing to adduce the secondary evidence has been entirely proper. Where, however, the party entitled to claim privilege permitted the party wishing to adduce the secondary evidence to inspect the relevant document in the course of disclosure under Part 31 of the Civil Procedure Rules 1998, then the latter party is normally entitled to assume that there has been a waiver of privilege (*Guiness Peat Properties Ltd v Fitzroy Robinson Partnership*). Exceptionally, however, even in these circumstances an injunction may be granted where inspection was obtained by fraud, where the party obtaining inspection or his solicitors realised that they were only permitted to inspect the relevant document in consequence of a mistake or where the mistake would have been obvious to the reasonable solicitor (*Guiness Peat Properties Ltd v Fitzroy Robinson Partnership; Pizzy v Ford Motor Company* (1994)). Moreover, it should be noted that CPR 31.20 provides that where a party was permitted to inspect a privileged document in consequence of the inadvertence of another party, the inspecting party may only use the privileged document or its contents with the court's permission (though normal practice appears to remain to apply promptly for an injunction (*Breeze v John Stacey* (1999))).

[*Note:* it appears that an injunction will not be granted to prevent the prosecution from making use of secondary evidence in criminal proceedings (*Butler v Board of Trade* (1971)). In such circumstances the court might, however, be prepared to exclude the secondary evidence in the exercise of its exclusionary discretion under s.78 of the Police and Criminal Evidence Act 1984.]

Are there exceptional circumstances in which a claim of legal professional privilege cannot be maintained?

(1) It was formerly believed that a claim of legal professional privilege would not be upheld where a defendant to criminal proceedings established on the balance of probabilities that the person claiming privilege no longer had an interest to protect and that the defendant did have a legitimate interest in adducing the privileged information in evidence. The House of Lords has now made clear, however, that a court cannot order the disclosure of privileged information in such circumstances, it being for the party entitled to claim the privilege to decide whether he wishes to waive it (*R. v Derby Magistrates' Court Ex p. B* (1995)).

(2) It appears that a party may not be entitled to claim legal professional privilege arising from confidential communications between lawyer or client and third party (*i.e.* litigation privilege) either in the context of wardship proceedings or in the context of proceedings under the Children Act 1989 (see, respectively, *Re A* (1991) and *Re L*

(*a minor*) (1996)). More fundamentally, it appears that
litigation privilege does not arise in the context of non-
adversarial proceedings (*Re L* (*a minor*)).

(3) It appears that where the purpose of confidential communications was to facilitate the commission of criminal
or fraudulent activity, the client cannot maintain the
privilege even though neither the legal adviser nor the
client were aware of the criminal or fraudulent purpose
(*R. v Central Criminal Court Ex p. Francis and Francis*
(1989)).

(4) Exceptionally, the privilege may be removed by statute
(*Jones v Searle* (1978)).

PUBLIC INTEREST IMMUNITY

What is the effect of public interest immunity?

Essentially, successfully claiming public interest immunity may
entitle a party to civil or criminal proceedings to withhold
disclosure or inspection of documents or to refuse to answer
questions. In civil proceedings, under Part 31 of the Civil
Procedure Rules 1998, a party may claim the right to withhold
inspection of a document (such that the other party knows that
the document exists but cannot obtain inspection of it) or may
even apply for permission to withhold disclosure of the document (such that the other party will not even know that the
document exists). In criminal proceedings (under the Crown
Court (Criminal Procedure and Investigations Act 1996) (Disclosure) Rules 1997, the prosecution may seek to claim public
interest immunity at an *ex parte* hearing without notifying the
defence, may seek to claim public interest immunity at an *ex
parte* hearing having notified the defence that an application is
being made or may seek to claim public interest immunity at an
inter partes hearing, having notified the defence of the nature of
the relevant material. The former of these three procedures is
appropriate where the fact that an application is being made
would in itself reveal to the defence the information to which
the public interest immunity claim relates and the second
procedure is appropriate where revealing the nature of the
relevant material would reveal to the defence the information to
which the public interest immunity claim relates. Where the
prosecution seek to adopt the former or second of these procedures, the court can direct them to adopt the second or first.

[*Note:* from April 2005 it appears that the relevant Crown Court and Magistrates' Courts rules will be found in the new Criminal Procedure Rules.]

Who can claim public interest immunity?

It is not merely central government which may claim public interest immunity, rather, other bodies, such as police forces, local authorities and even the National Society for the Prevention of Cruelty to Children, have also made successful claims (*D v National Society for the Prevention of Cruelty to Children* (1978)).

When will a public interest immunity claim succeed?

A public interest immunity claim may either take the form of a contents claim (*i.e.* a claim that disclosing the particular document is against the public interest) or a class claim (*i.e.* a claim that the document falls within a class of documents the production of which is against the public interest). In practice, central government will no longer make class claims but will only claim public interest immunity if disclosing the particular document could cause real damage to the public interest.

In determining whether a public interest immunity claim is successful, the court is required to balance the public interest against disclosure with the public interest in favour of disclosure (*Conway v Rimmer* (1968)). The public interest against disclosure might, for example, take the form of potential damage to national security, such as revealing plans of secret weapons during a war (*Duncan v Cammell Laird* (1942)) or that of revealing the identity of an informant (whether an informant to the police or to some other body, such as the National Society for the Prevention of Cruelty to Children (*D v National Society for the Prevention of Cruelty to Children*). Essentially, the public interest in favour of disclosure is that of doing justice in the proceedings before the court. Thus, for example, where withholding the identity of a police informant might prevent a person charged with a serious criminal offence from proving his innocence, it is likely that the court will order disclosure on the basis that the public interest against disclosure is outweighed by the public interest in favour of disclosure (*R. v Keane* (1994)).

The result of a public interest immunity claim will not necessarily be that the court either orders full disclosure of the relevant material or orders its non disclosure. Rather, in appropriate circumstances, the court may be prepared to order an appropriate form of limited disclosure (*R. v H* (2004)).

Is the court entitled to inspect the documents before reaching its decision?

The court is entitled to inspect the documents to which a public interest immunity claim relates before deciding whether the claim is successful (*Conway v Rimmer*) and will normally do so in the context of criminal proceedings (*R. v Douglas* (1993)).

Is there a right to waive public interest immunity?

Unlike privilege there is no right to waive public interest immunity because, where it arises, the evidence to which it relates is rendered inadmissible. In practice, however, where the party who is entitled to claim public interest immunity (*e.g.* a government minister) does not believe that it is in the public interest to do so, this will be a matter which the court will take into account when balancing the public interest against disclosure with the public interest in favour of disclosure, and which may well persuade the court that the relevant material should be disclosed (*R. v Chief Constable of West Midlands Police Ex p. Wiley* (1995)).

Human Rights

Where the prosecution withhold disclosure of material evidence for or against the accused, this may give rise to a violation of Art.6 of the European Convention on Human Rights (*Rowe and Davis v UK* (2000)). This, it appears, will be the case either if withholding disclosure is not strictly necessary or if the procedures adopted by the court fail to satisfy the requirements of a fair trial. Where a public interest immunity claim follows the procedure which is now laid down under the Crown Court (Criminal Procedure and Investigations Act 1996) (Disclosure) Rules 1997, however, and withholding disclosure on public interest grounds is strictly necessary, it appears that withholding disclosure is unlikely to give rise to a violation of Art.6 (see *Jasper v UK* (2000); *Fitt v UK* (2000)).

In exceptional circumstances, in order to ensure that the accused is given a fair trial, it may be necessary for the court to order that "special counsel" be appointed to represent the interests of the accused in the context of a public interest immunity claim (*R. v H* (2004). It should be noted, however, that special counsel is not responsible to the accused. Moreover, special counsel must not disclose the material which the public interest immunity claims concerns to the accused.

---

8. ESTOPPEL BY RECORD AND THE USE OF PREVIOUS CONVICTIONS AND JUDICIAL FINDINGS AS EVIDENCE OF THE FACTS UPON WHICH THEY WERE BASED

In this chapter we will consider both the operation of the doctrine of *res judicata* (estoppel by record) in civil and criminal proceedings and the extent to which previous convictions and judicial findings in civil cases may be adduced as evidence of the facts upon which they were based in proceedings between parties other than the parties to the proceedings in which the accused was convicted or the findings were made.

THE DOCTRINE OF *RES JUDICATA* IN CIVIL PROCEEDINGS

Is the judgment of a civil court conclusive evidence against all persons of the facts upon which it was based?

The judgment of a civil court is conclusive evidence against all persons of "the state of things which it actually effects" but not of the findings on which it is based (*Hollington v Hewthorn* (1943)). Thus, for example, if a court awards P £10,000 damages against D in consequence of D's breach of contract, the judgment conclusively proves that P was awarded £10,000 damages against D but does not conclusively prove that D breached his contract with P.

Where the judgment of a civil court does not merely determine the interests of the parties to it (*i.e.* whether one is liable in damages for breach of contract or in negligence to the other) but, rather, determines the "status" of a person or thing, however, then such status is determined conclusively as against all persons. For example, a decree of nullity is conclusive evidence against all persons of the invalidity of the relevant marriage (*Salvesen v The Administrator of Austrian Property* (1927)). A judgment of the former type (*e.g.* one which merely determines liability in Tort or Contract) is termed a judgment *in personam*. A judgment of the latter type (*i.e.* one which determines status) is termed a judgment *in rem*.

Are parties to civil proceedings ever estopped from re-litigating findings made by a court in the course of civil proceedings between them?

A party to civil proceedings or his privies may be estopped from re-litigating findings made by a court in the course of civil proceedings between himself or his privies and another party or his privies. This form of estoppel is known as estoppel by record or estopped *per rem judicatam* and, as is the case with estoppels generally, will only take effect if pleaded (*i.e.* if set out in the party's Statement of Case) (*Vooght v Winch* (1819)). Such an estoppel may either take the form of a cause of action estoppel (preventing the re-litigation of a previously litigated cause of action) or that of an issue estoppel (preventing the re-litigation of an issue which formed an essential element of a previously litigated cause of action).

Thus, where P successfully sued D, a builder, for damages in respect of D's breach of a contract to complete a building in a "good and workmanlike manner", P could not, by bringing subsequent proceedings in respect of the same cause of action against D, recover further damages arising from consequences of D's defective workmanship which P had not particularised for the purposes of the original action (*Conquer v Boot* (1928)).

Again, where, in legal proceedings brought by P's passenger T, P and D had been found equally liable in negligence in respect of the car crash in which T had been injured, P was, in the course of subsequent proceedings brought by P against D, estopped (an issue estoppel) from asserting other than that he was fifty per cent contributorily negligent, the issue having been determined in the course of the proceedings brought by T (*Wall v Radford* (1991)).

What conditions must be satisfied in order for a cause of action estoppel or an issue estoppel to arise?

A cause of action estoppel or an issue estoppel may arise only if the following requirements are satisfied:

(1) The parties to the latter proceedings must be (or be the privies of) the parties to the original proceedings.

Thus, P was not estopped from denying contributory negligence in an action which he brought against D concerning injuries which P had suffered in a vehicle collision even though D had previously proved contributory negligence in an action brought against D by P's father, who owned the car which P had been driving, in respect of the damage to his car (*Townsend v Bishop* (1939)).

[*Note:* at the time when Townsend's case was decided, contributory negligence provided a complete defence to liability and consequently had P been estopped from denying contributory negligence his action must have failed.]

(2) The parties to the latter proceedings must be litigating in the same capacities in which they litigated the original proceedings.

Thus, where, in legal proceedings brought by T, P and D had been found equally to blame for a collision between vehicles in which T's property had been damaged, P, litigating in the capacity of personal representative of his wife (who had been killed in the collision), was not estopped, in the course of subsequent proceedings against D, from denying contributory negligence (*Marginson v Blackburn B.C.* (1939)). P was, however, estopped from denying contributory negligence when litigating on his own behalf.

[*Note:* at the time when Marginson's case was decided, contributory negligence provided a complete defence to liability and consequently the effect of the estoppel was that P could not bring his personal action against D though he could bring the action on behalf of his wife's estate.]

(3) The cause of action or issue which is being litigated in the latter proceedings must have been determined in the original proceedings.

In *Wall v Radford* (considered above), Popplewell J. held that, for the purpose of determining whether P was estopped from denying that he was 50 per cent contributorily negligent, the factual issues raised in the subsequent proceedings were the same as those which had been determined in the original proceedings. His Lordship declined to follow earlier authority to the effect that where the subsequent proceedings involve consideration of legal duties of care different from those which the original proceedings concerned, the issues raised in the subsequent proceedings are not the same as those determined in the earlier proceedings (*Bell v Holmes* (1956)).

[*Note:* in exceptional circumstances a party may not be prevented, by issue estoppel, from re-opening a previously litigated issue. Such circumstances include those in which new evidence has become admissible which could not, by exercising reasonable diligence, have been adduced in the original proceedings and those in which, following the original proceedings, there has been a change in the law (*Arnold v National Westminster Bank* (1991)).]

In *Conquer v Boot* (considered above), the plaintiff was debarred from bringing a second action in respect of the same cause of action. In contrast, in *Brunsden v Humphrey* (1884), a cab driver was not debarred from bringing an action to recover damages for personal injuries which he had sustained in an accident by virtue of the fact that he had already recovered damages from the same defendant in earlier proceedings concerning damage to his cab resulting from the same accident. This was so as the two actions concerned two distinct causes of action.

(4) The court which determined the relevant issue in the original proceedings must have been a court of competent jurisdiction and must have given a final judgment upon the merits.

The decision of a court or tribunal which does not determine a dispute between contending parties cannot become conclusive evidence of the facts upon which it was based against the parties to subsequent civil proceedings, the court or tribunal not being a "court of competent jurisdiction" (*The European Gateway* (1987)). Moreover, even where the decision of a court or tribunal does determine a dispute between contending parties, its decision will not become conclusive evidence of the facts upon which it was based against the parties to subsequent civil proceedings if the court or tribunal did not possess jurisdiction to finally determine the relevant issue (*R. v Hutchings* (1881)).

[*Note:* the fact that it is possible to appeal from the decision of a court or tribunal does not prevent its decision from being final for this purpose.]

Should a party to legal proceedings pursue every cause of action available to him?

Where a party to legal proceedings seeks to brings a claim or to raise a defence which he could have brought in the context of earlier proceedings, the court may (under what is commonly referred to as "the rule in *Henderson v Henderson*") be prepared to strike out the claim or the defence as an abuse of process. The court may be prepared to do this if the other party to the proceedings persuades the court that the claim or defence should have been brought or raised in the earlier proceedings (*Johnson v Gore Wood* (2001)). Whether the court is prepared to strike out a claim or defence on this basis will depend upon factors such as the reason why the claim or defence was not litigated in the earlier proceedings (*e.g.* whether the claimant was aware of the facts underlying the second claim at the time of the original litigation).

Examples of factual situation in which the court might, in appropriate circumstances, be prepared to strike out a claim as an abuse of process under the rule in *Henderson v Henderson* (1843) are (as the Court of Appeal recognised in *Talbot v Berkshire CC* (1994)) provided by the facts of *Brunsden v Humphrey* and *Wall v Radford* (both seen above).

THE ADMISSIBILITY OF PREVIOUS CONVICTIONS AND JUDICIAL FINDINGS AS EVIDENCE OF THE FACTS UPON WHICH THEY WERE BASED IN CIVIL PROCEEDINGS BETWEEN PARTIES OTHER THAN THE PARTIES TO THE PROCEEDINGS IN WHICH THE ACCUSED WAS CONVICTED OR THE FINDINGS WERE MADE

The effect of the decision of the Court of Appeal in *Hollington v Hewthorn* was that previous convictions and judicial findings were not admissible as evidence of the facts upon which they were based in civil proceedings between parties other than the parties to the proceedings in which the accused was convicted or the findings were made. Thus, in *Hollington v Hewthorn*, in which P's car was damaged in a collision with a car driven by D, P was not entitled to adduce evidence of D's previous conviction for careless driving as evidence of D's negligence. The ambit of the rule in *Hollington v Hewthorn* in civil proceedings has, however, been substantially reduced by ss.11, 12 and 13 of the Civil Evidence Act 1968. Other than in relation to adultery and paternity (which are considered below), however, the rule still applies so as to render a civil judgment inadmissible in subsequent criminal or civil proceedings as evidence of the findings made by the court (*R. v D* (1996); *Secretary of State for Trade and Industry v Bairstow* (2004)).

Collateral attacks

It may be an abuse of process (and thus result in a claim being struck out) for a claimant (or in some circumstances a defendant) to challenge a judicial decision by a parallel judicial process (*i.e.* via a collateral attack). Thus, for example, where an accused whose criminal appeal is unsuccessful brings a civil claim for damages against a police force as a means of challenging his criminal conviction "by the back door", the claim may be struck out on this basis (*Hunter v Chief Constable of the West Midlands Police* (1982)).

The admissibility of previous convictions in civil proceedings

Essentially, s.11(1) of the Civil Evidence Act 1968 provides that a person's subsisting conviction is admissible in civil proceedings to prove that the person committed the offence of which he was convicted provided that proving that the relevant person committed the relevant offence is relevant to an issue before the court. The section also provides that where a person's conviction is admitted under the section, then the person shall be taken to have committed the offence of which he was convicted unless the contrary is proved.

[*Note:* a conviction is subsisting unless and until it has been quashed—*Re Raphael* (1973).]

Thus, were the facts of *Hollington v Hewthorn* to arise today, D's conviction would not merely be admissible as evidence of his negligence but, moreover, D would be presumed to have driven carelessly unless he proved that he had not done so. Thus, D would bear the legal burden of proving on the balance of probabilities that he did not commit the offence of which he was convicted (*Mccauley v Hope* (1999)). What is unclear, however, is whether the effect of s.11 is merely to place the burden of proving that he did not commit the offence on D or whether, additionally, a conviction which is admitted under s.11 acts as evidence proving that D did, in fact, commit the relevant offence (*Stupple v Royal Insurance Co Ltd* (1971)). Whichever view is correct, it does appear that the task of rebutting the presumption that the person convicted of an offence in fact committed it is, in general, not an easy one to accomplish (*Hunter v Chief Constable of the West Midlands Police*).

[*Note:* where a party intends to adduce evidence of a previous conviction under s.11 the Civil Procedure Rules 1998 provide that he must include a statement of such intent in the particulars of claim.]

Finally, it should be noted that where the commission of a criminal offence by the claimant is relevant to an issue in proceedings for libel or slander, the claimant's subsisting conviction for the relevant offence is, under s.13 of the Civil Evidence Act 1968, admissible as *conclusive evidence* that he committed it.

The admissibility of previous findings of adultery and paternity in civil proceedings

Essentially, s.12 of the Civil Evidence Act 1968 provides that subsisting findings of adultery made in matrimonial proceedings in the High Court or in a County Court, subsisting findings of paternity and subsisting adjudications of paternity in affiliation proceedings are admissible in civil proceedings as evidence of adultery or paternity provided that proving that the relevant person committed the relevant adultery or fathered the relevant child is relevant to an issue before the court. The section also provides that where a finding or adjudication is admitted under the section then the person who was found guilty of the relevant adultery or was found to be the father of the relevant child shall be taken to have committed the relevant adultery or to have fathered the relevant child unless the contrary is proved.

THE DOCTRINE OF *RES JUDICATA* IN CRIMINAL PROCEEDINGS

Can a person who has been convicted or acquitted of a criminal offence be subsequently tried for that offence?

A person who has been convicted of a criminal offence may plead *autrefois convict* in order to bar subsequent proceedings for the same offence against him. Similarly, a person who has been acquitted of a criminal offence may plead *autrefois acquit* in order to bar subsequent proceedings for the same offence against him. Further, the plea of *autre fois convict* and *autre fois acquit* also bar proceedings against a person in respect of lesser offences of which he would have been convicted in earlier proceedings when charged with a more serious offence. Authority for the above propositions is provided by *DPP v Connelly* (1964). Moreover, it may be an abuse of process to bring proceedings against a person for an offence of which he could not have been convicted in earlier proceedings if the later proceedings concern substantially the same facts as the earlier proceedings. (*DPP v Connelly; R. v Beedie* (1997)). It should be noted, however, that, under Part 10 of the Criminal Justice Act 2003, there will, in future, be circumstances in which the Court of Appeal will, in the interests of justice, be required to quash a person's conviction and order a retrial in the context of offences such as murder, kidnapping and rape.

Can the prosecution dispute a previous acquittal in subsequent criminal proceedings?

As was seen above, where proceedings concern an offence of which the accused has already been acquitted, the accused may plead *autrefois acquit*. Where, however, proceedings concern an offence of which the accused could not have been convicted in earlier proceedings and do not concern substantially the same facts as the earlier proceedings, the doctrine of *autrefois* does not apply and, moreover, there is no abuse of process. In such circumstances, and subject both to the operation of the rules of evidence which regulate the admissibility of evidence of bad character (see Chapter 13 below) and to the exercise of the court's exclusionary discretion under s.78 of the Police and Criminal Evidence Act 1984 (see Chapter 11 below), the prosecution can, if this is relevant to an issue in the proceedings, dispute a previous acquittal of the accused (*R. v Z* (2000)). Thus, for example, where the accused is charged with rape, evidence concerning his previous acquittals for rape may be admissible for the prosecution even though the evidence contradicts the correctness of the previous acquittals (*R. v Z*), (though he may not be re-tried for an alleged rape for which he has previously been acquitted unless his conviction has been quashed under Part 10 of the 2003 Act).

Can an issue estoppel lie in criminal proceedings?

In *R. v Humphreys* (1977) the House of Lords held that an issue estoppel cannot lie in criminal proceedings. Thus, during Humphrey's trial for perjury, a police officer was properly permitted to testify that he had seen Humphreys driving a motor vehicle in 1972 even though the police officer had previously testified to the same effect during a trial at the end of which Humphreys was acquitted of driving a motor vehicle whilst disqualified.

THE ADMISSIBILITY OF PREVIOUS CONVICTIONS AS EVIDENCE OF THE FACTS UPON WHICH THEY WERE BASED IN CRIMINAL PROCEEDINGS BETWEEN PARTIES OTHER THAN THE PARTIES TO THE PROCEEDINGS IN WHICH THE ACCUSED WAS CONVICTED

The ambit of the rule in *Hollington v Hewthorn* (see above) in criminal proceedings has been reduced by s.74 of the Police and Criminal Evidence Act 1984. Essentially, s.74(1) (as amended by the Criminal Justice Act 2003) provides that a person's previous conviction is admissible in criminal proceedings in which he is not the accused to prove that the person committed the offence of which he was convicted if evidence that the person committed the offence is admissible. Section 74(2) provides that where a conviction is admitted under the section, then the person convicted shall be taken to have committed the offence of which he was convicted unless the contrary is proved.

[*Note:* the conviction must be a subsisting conviction, *i.e.* one which has not been quashed—s.75(4)).]

In order for a conviction to be admissible under s.74(1) it appears that evidence that the relevant person committed the relevant offence must be admissible under the bad character provisions of the Criminal Justice Act 2003 (see Chapter 13, below). Even where such evidence is admissible, however, it seems that the trial judge may find it necessary to exclude evidence of the conviction in the exercise of his discretion under s.78 of the 1984 Act upon the basis that its admission would have such an adverse effect on the fairness of the proceedings that it ought not to be admitted (*R. v O'Connor* (1987)). This may be necessary (for example, in the context of a conspiracy trial) in circumstances in which the jury might infer if the conviction was admitted that because the relevant person (*e.g.* a conspirator who pleaded guilty) committed the offence of which he was convicted, the logical conclusion was automatically that the accused (*e.g.* a conspirator who pleaded not guilty) was guilty of the offence with which he was charged. Moreover, where a conviction is admitted under s.74, the judge should explain to the jury why it has been admitted (*R. v Kempster* (1990)).

Finally, s.74(3) essentially provides that where evidence that the accused has committed an offence is admissible (*i.e.* under the bad character provisions of the Criminal Justice Act 2003), if the accused is proved to have been convicted of the relevant offence, he shall be taken to have committed the offence unless the contrary is proved.

Human Rights

It appears that the admission for the prosecution of a conviction of a person other than the accused under s.74(1) in the context of a proper exercise by the judge of his exclusionary discretion and the giving of an appropriate direction by the judge to the jury in circumstances in which the accused could have called the person whose conviction was admitted under s.74(1) to give defence evidence will not give rise to a violation of Art.6(1) of the European Convention on Human Rights (*MH v UK* (1997)).

9. THE HEARSAY RULE AND ITS COMMON LAW EXCEPTIONS IN CRIMINAL PROCEEDINGS

[*Note:* this chapter is written as though the evidence provisions of the Criminal Justice Act 2003 are already in force. The relevant provisions are due to be brought into force in 2005.]

Basically, the effect of s.114(1) of the Criminal Justice Act 2003 is that a statement which was not made in oral evidence in the proceedings (*i.e.* a hearsay statement) is only admissible in criminal proceedings: where statute makes the hearsay evidence admissible; where a common law exception to the hearsay rule which has been preserved by s.118 of the Criminal Justice Act 2003 makes it admissible; where the parties agree to its admission; or where the court admits it in the exercise of the inclusionary discretion conferred upon it by s.114(1)(d) of the 2003 Act. The admissibility of hearsay statements as confessions under s.76 of the Police and Criminal Evidence Act 1984 is considered in Chapter 11 below. The admission of hearsay evidence in criminal proceedings under other statutory exceptions to the hearsay rule or in the exercise of the court's inclusionary discretion and the various safeguards which the 2003 Act imposes are considered in Chapter 12 below. The present chapter is concerned both with the nature of those circumstances in which a statement is a hearsay statement (and thus will be inadmissible in criminal proceedings unless a hearsay exception applies) and with the nature of some of the common law exceptions to the hearsay rule which s.118 of the 2003 Act preserves.

To what types of statement does the hearsay rule apply?

The hearsay rule, as it applies in the context of criminal proceedings, applies to statements as defined by s.115(2) of the Criminal Justice Act 2003. Section 115(2) defines a statement as ". . . any representation of fact or opinion made by a person by whatever means; and it includes a representation made in a sketch, photofit or other pictorial form.". Thus, the hearsay rule applies to written statements, to oral statements and to statements made by conduct. The effect of s.114(1), however, is that a statement is only a hearsay statement if the statement was not made in oral evidence in the proceedings *and* is relied on in those proceedings as evidence of a matter stated.

Written statements For example, the hearsay rule applied at common law (and will presumably apply under the 2003 Act) where the prosecution, in order to identify certain cars, wished to rely upon written records kept by a car manufacturer which identified the cars by reference to numbers on their engines (*Myers v DPP* (1965)). Consequently, the records were not admissible in evidence.

[*Note:* such records would now be admissible in evidence both in civil and in criminal proceedings under statutory exceptions to the hearsay rule; see Chapters 10 and 12 below.]

Oral statements For example, the hearsay rule applied at common law (and will presumably apply under the 2003 Act) where the prosecution, in order to prove that the accused had murdered the deceased, wished to rely on an oral statement made by the deceased shortly after he was attacked in which he named his attackers (*R. v Andrews* (1987)).

[*Note:* the statement was admissible under a common law exception to the hearsay rule which is considered in the course of the present chapter.]

Statements made by conduct For example, the hearsay rule applied at common law (and will presumably apply under the 2003 Act) where the prosecution, in order to prove that the accused had murdered the deceased, wished to rely upon a statement made by the deceased by gesture after her throat had been cut by which she identified the accused as the man who had cut her throat (*R. v Chandrasekera* (1937)).

[*Note:* the statement was admissible under a statutory exception to the hearsay rule.]

Statements made in other legal proceedings For example, the hearsay rule applied at common law (and will presumably apply under the 2003 Act) so as to prevent the admission in subsequent legal proceedings as evidence of the place of a pauper's last legal settlement of a written and signed examination of the pauper, the pauper having been examined in court several years earlier for the purpose of determining the place of his last legal settlement (*R. v The Inhabitants of Eriswell* (1790)).

[*Note:* statements made by witnesses in earlier legal proceedings may now be admissible under statutory exceptions to the hearsay rule.]

Sketches and photofits The definition of "statement" in s.115(2) of the Criminal Justice Act 2003 makes clear that, unlike the position at common law (*R. v Cook* (1987), the hearsay rule is applicable to statements in the form of sketches and photofits which are relied on as evidence of matters stated. In practice, sketches and photofits may well be be admissible under one or more of the exceptions to the hearsay rule which the 2003 Act creates or preserves.

To what types of statement does the hearsay rule not apply?

Implied statements Section 115(3) of the Criminal Justice Act 2003 essentially provides that the hearsay provisions of the 2003 Act only apply to a matter stated if the purpose (or at least one of the purposes) of the person making the statement appears to the court to have been either to cause another person to believe the matter or to cause another person to act or a machine to operate upon the basis that the matter is as stated. The effect of this provision is, essentially, that (unlike the former position at common law), implied statements do not amount to hearsay statements if it appears that their maker did not make them for either or both of the abovementioned purposes. Thus, for example, if statements made by persons during telephone calls to the accused's house asking for the accused and asking for drugs are tendered by the prosecution in order to prove that the accused deals in drugs, the statements will not be hearsay statements provided that the persons making the calls neither did so for the purpose of making another person believe that he was a drugs dealer nor did so for the purpose of causing a person to act or a machine to operate upon that basis. At common law, such statements would have been hearsay statements even if they were made for neither of these purposes (*R. v Kearley* (1992)).

Representations which were not made by persons The definition of "statement" in s.115(2) of the Criminal Justice Act 2003 only applies to representations made by persons. Thus, the hearsay rule does not apply to representations which were not made by persons; *i.e.* it does not apply to representations which were made by machines. Where a machine makes a representation but the representation depends for its accuracy on information which was supplied by a person, the effect of s.129(1) of the 2003 Act is, however, that the representation is not admissible as evidence of the fact represented unless it is proved that the information was accurate. In contrast, where a machine makes a representation without relying upon information supplied by a human, the s.129(1) requirement will not apply.

The purpose for which the statement is tendered The hearsay rule does not apply where a statement is relied upon other than as evidence of a matter stated (see s.114(1) of the Criminal Justice Act 2003). Thus, for example, the rule did not apply at common law (and presumably will not apply under the 2003 Act) where the accused, whose defence was duress, wished to repeat in court threats made to him by terrorists (*Subramanian v Public Prosecutor* (1956)). The rule did not apply because, in the context of the defence of duress, the statements were relevant regardless of whether they were true (in the sense that the terrorists actually intended to carry out the threats which they made) or false (in the sense that the terrorists had lied to the accused and did not intend to carry out the threats). Rather, what was important in that context was whether the threats had been made (which depended upon the truth of the accused's testimony in court and not upon that of the terrorist's statements). This was so because if the threats had been made and believed by the accused, they were potentially capable of amounting to duress whether or not there was, in reality, any intention to carry them out.

Photographs, video recordings and films   At common law it was clear that the hearsay rule did not apply to photographs or video recordings of persons, places or events (see for example, *Taylor v Chief Constable of Cheshire* (1987)). It is submitted that this will continue to be the case under the Criminal Justice Act 2003 as the content of such photographs, recordings or films will not amount to "statements" for the purposes of the 2003 Act, they are not amounting to "representations of fact or opinion made by a person" (s.115(2)). In contrast, however, it is submitted that a photograph, film or video recording of a document written by a person, of a statement made by a person by conduct, or of an audio recording of words spoken by a person does amount to a hearsay statement if relied upon as evidence of a matter stated.

MAJOR COMMON LAW EXCEPTIONS TO THE HEARSAY RULE

Where a hearsay statement falls within an exception to the hearsay rule the statement is admissible in evidence even though it is a hearsay statement. The Criminal Justice Act 2003 abolishes certain common law exceptions to the hearsay rule, such as the dying declaration, but preserves a number of others. Examination of all of the preserved common law hearsay exceptions falls outside the scope of the present book. Rather, the examples of preserved common law hearsay exceptions which we will consider are the four categories of hearsay statement which are commonly said to be admissible in criminal proceedings because they "form part of the *res gestae*".

Statements forming part of the *res gestae*

[*Note:* it appears that these common law hearsay exceptions apply only in criminal proceedings as they have not been preserved by s.7 of the Civil Evidence Act 1995 (see Chapter 10 below). In the context of criminal proceedings they are preserved by s.118(1)4 of the Criminal Justice Act 2003.]

Statements which are closely associated with an act or state of affairs the performance or existence of which is of relevance in legal proceedings may be admissible in those proceedings as evidence of matters stated. Essentially, a statement may be so admissible either if it concerns its maker's contemporaneous actions, physical sensations or mental state or if it is closely associated with a dramatic event.

Statements concerning the contemporaneous actions, physical sensations or mental state of their maker
A statement explaining its maker's actions which was made at the time when the relevant actions were performed may be admissible to prove why they were performed. Thus, if a person, whilst away from home, writes a letter explaining why he is staying away from home, the letter may be admissible to prove why he stayed away from home, should this be of relevance to an issue before the court (*Rouch v Great Western Railway Co* (1841)). Moreover, it has been held that where a witness cannot remember whom he identified at an identification parade, a police officer who attended the parade can repeat in court the statement which the witness made at the time identifying the accused, the statement accompanying and explaining the activities of seeing and recognising (*R. v McKay* (1990)).

A statement concerning its maker's physical sensations which was made at the time when he experienced the relevant sensations is admissible to prove that he experienced the relevant sensations but is not admissible as evidence of their cause. Thus, if a patient, whilst being examined by a doctor, tells the doctor that he has a pain in his leg and also tells the doctor that the pain was caused by an insect sting, the doctor may repeat the statement in court for the purpose of proving that the patient was in pain but may not do so for the purpose of proving that the patient had been stung by an insect (*Amys v Barton* (1911)). Moreover, where a patient is ill for several days, a statement made several days into the period of illness may be admissible to prove that the illness had been on-going from the date of its commencement (*Aveson v Lord Kinnaird* (1805)).

Finally, a statement concerning its maker's mental state at the time when he made the statement is admissible to prove what its maker intended to do or believed to be the case at that time but is not admissible as evidence of the truth of its maker's beliefs. Thus, where a man states that he is insolvent, his statement may be repeated in court to prove that he was aware of his insolvency but the fact of his insolvency must be proved by other admissible evidence (*Thomas v Connell* (1838)).

A statement of intent may be admissible whether it was made at the time when the intended act was carried out or whether it was made prior to performance of that act, in which case the court may be entitled to infer that the intent was still possessed by the maker at the relevant time (*R. v Moghal* (1977)). The longer the time gap between the making of the statement and the performance of the act, however, the lower the probative value of the statement, if it is admitted in evidence, will be. Moreover, if the statement was made after the performance of the relevant act, a court will be unlikely to admit it if the time gap was substantial (*R. v Moghal*).

[*Note:* it is unclear whether a statement of intent may be admitted in evidence to prove that the act which its maker intended to perform was, in fact, carried out by him. There is authority both for and against his proposition (see, respectively, *R. v Buckley* (1873) and *R. v Wainwright* (1875)). It is also unclear whether statements concerning their maker's state of mind are admissible because they fall within a common law exception to the hearsay rule or whether such statements are not hearsay statements at all (see, for example, *R. v Gilfoyle* (1996)).]

Statements closely associated with a dramatic event
Statements closely associated with a dramatic event are admissible as evidence of matters stated if the possibility that they have been concocted or distorted can be disregarded. In other words, to adopt the wording of s.118(1)4(a) of the Criminal Justice Act

2003, a statement is admissible as evidence of matters stated if its maker was ". . . so emotionally overpowered by an event that the possibility of concoction or distortion can be disregarded". As the House of Lords made clear in *R. v Andrews* (1987), the judge must determine whether this is so by considering whether the maker's mind was so dominated by the event at the time when the statement was made that the possibility of concoction or distortion can be ruled out. The judge must take into account any factors which might increase the risk of concoction or distortion, such as whether the maker had a motive to concoct or distort. Moreover, the judge should consider any factors which give rise to a particular risk of error. For example, where the statement relates to an identification which the maker made, it may be that the identification was made in circumstances in which the reliability of identification evidence would be doubtful (*e.g.* a fleeting glimpse of a person a long way away in the dark). Finally, if the judge decides that the statement is admissible, he should still draw the jury's attention to factors which might increase the risk of concoction or distortion or which might give rise to a particular risk of error and direct them that they must be satisfied that there was no concoction or distortion.

In *Andrews'* case, the question before the House of Lords was whether a statement made by a murder victim identifying the accused as the murderer had properly been admitted in evidence. The statement had been made by Andrews a few minutes after he was fatally stabbed. The statement had been admitted by the trial judge even though there was evidence to suggest that Andrews had a motive to concoct evidence against the accused and even though the possibility of error was increased because Andrews had been drinking heavily. The House of Lords held that, upon the facts of the case, the trial judge had been entitled to decide that there was no possibility of concoction or distortion and, consequently, that the evidence had properly been admitted.

In order for a statement to be admitted under this exception to the hearsay rule, it is necessary that the existence of the dramatic event and that the statement was made in its context are both proved by evidence other than the content of the statement itself (*R. v Rattan* (1972)). Where, for example, the relevant statement was a request for the police made to a telephone operator by an hysterical woman, the Privy Council held that evidence that the statement was closely associated with a dramatic event was provided by the fact that the accused's wife had been shot and killed in the house from which the call was made a few minutes after it was made, by the fact that she made the statement in a call requesting the police and by her tone of voice when she made the call (*R. v Rattan*).

It should be noted that a statement may be admitted under this exception to the hearsay rule even though the maker of the statement is available to be called though, where the hearsay evidence is tendered by the prosecution, the court may, in such circumstances, find it necessary to exclude the hearsay in the exercise of its exclusionary discretion (*i.e.* under s.78 of the Police and Criminal Evidence Act 1984) so as to give the accused the possibility of cross-examining the relevant witness (*Attorney General's Reference (No.1 of 2003)*). It should also be noted that a statement may be admitted under this exception to the hearsay rule whether it was made by the victim of a crime, by a third party or even by the accused (see, for example, *R. v Glover* (1991)).

HUMAN RIGHTS

The admission of hearsay evidence for the prosecution may, in appropriate circumstances, be capable of giving rise to a violation of Art.6 of the European Convention on Human Rights. This is so because Art.6(3)(d) gives the accused the right to examine, or to have examined, the witness against him. Admitting hearsay evidence for the prosecution will not automatically have this effect. Rather, in determining whether the admission of hearsay evidence for the prosecution will have this effect, it appears that the court should take into account matters such as whether the hearsay evidence forms the sole or main evidence of the accused's guilt, whether the defence have had the opportunity to adduce other evidence contradicting the hearsay evidence and whether the defence have had an opportunity to discredit the maker of the hearsay statement (*Triverdi v UK* (1997)). If admitting hearsay evidence for the prosecution would give rise to a violation of Art.6 then, it is submitted, in order to comply with the court's duty, under s.3 of the Human Rights Act 1998, to read and give effect to legislation, where possible, in a convention compatible way, the court should exercise its exclusionary discretion, under s.78 of the Police and Criminal Evidence Act 1984, so as to exclude the hearsay evidence (see, for example, *R. v H* (2003)).

10. CIVIL EVIDENCE ACT 1995

The Civil Evidence Act 1995 provides a statutory regime which makes hearsay evidence admissible in civil proceedings. The effect of the definition of "civil proceedings" in s.11 is, however, that the provisions of the Act do not apply to civil proceedings to which the strict rules of evidence are inapplicable (*e.g.* claims which have been allocated to the small claims track).

ADMISSIBILITY

Section 1 of the Civil Evidence Act 1995 makes hearsay evidence admissible in civil proceedings. Hearsay is defined by s.1 of the 1995 Act as ". . . a statement made otherwise than by a person while giving oral evidence in the proceedings which is tendered as evidence of the matters stated. . . " and a statement is ". . . any representation of fact or opinion, however made" (s.13)).

Section 14 provides, however, that s.1 does not make hearsay evidence admissible if the hearsay evidence is inadmissible for some reason other than its hearsay nature (*e.g.* if it is inadmissible due to the operation of some other rule of evidence, of some other statutory provision or rules of court). Thus, for example, hearsay evidence in the form of a representation of opinion will only be admissible if the rules concerning the admission of opinion evidence have been complied with (see Chapter 6 above).

Section 1 also provides that ss.2 to 6 of the 1995 Act (considered below) do not apply where hearsay evidence is admissible under some exception to the hearsay rule other than the general exception provided by s.1 (*e.g.* under a common law exception to the hearsay rule preserved by s.7, (considered below), or under an exception to the hearsay rule provided by some other statutory provision, such as the Children (Admissibility of Hearsay Evidence) Order 1993).

Hearsay notices

Section 2(1) of the Civil Evidence Act 1995 requires a party intending to adduce hearsay evidence in civil proceedings to give notice of this fact to the other parties to the proceedings and, if requested, to provide the other parties with further information concerning the hearsay evidence. The parties may, however, agree to dispense with the requirements of s.2(1) and a party entitled to receive a hearsay notice, etc., may waive his entitlement (s.2(3)). Moreover, s.2(1) only requires a party to comply with its requirements to the extent to which, in the circumstances, such compliance is reasonable and practicable in order to enable the other parties to deal with the relevant evidence in consequence of its hearsay nature. Further, it should be noted that the requirements of s.2(1) do not apply in relation to evidence at hearings other than trials or to affidavits or witness statements not containing hearsay evidence or to statements allegedly made by persons whose estates form the subject matter of probate actions (CPR 33.3).

The Civil Procedure Rules 1998 (CPR) make provision, for the purposes of s.2(1) of the Civil Evidence Act 1995, for the giving of notice of the fact that a party proposes to adduce hearsay evidence (CPR 33.2). If the party intends to call a witness to prove the hearsay statement, notice takes the form of the service of the witness's witness statement on the other parties. If the party intends to prove the hearsay statement by means of the witness statement of a witness whom he does not intend to call, then notice takes the form of the service of the witness's witness statement on the other parties but, in addition, the serving party must also inform the other parties that the witness is not being called and explain why this is so. If the hearsay statement is not to be proved in either of the abovementioned ways, then the party who wishes to rely upon it must serve a notice on the other parties identifying the hearsay evidence, stating that he intends to rely on it and giving the reason why the witness will not be called.

Where a party fails to comply with the requirements of s.2 this does not affect the admissibility of the hearsay evidence (s.2(4)). Such failure may, however, be taken into account by the court when determining the weight of the hearsay evidence, may result in an adjournment and may be of relevance when the court is exercising its powers in relation to costs. Further, it should be noted that where a party fails to serve a witness statement as required by rules of court, the oral evidence of the relevant witness is only admissible with the permission of the court (CPR 32.10). Thus, whilst failure to serve a hearsay notice does not affect the admissibility of hearsay evidence, failure to serve a witness statement in respect of the evidence of a witness which is to be used to prove a hearsay statement may render that witness's oral evidence inadmissible.

[*Note:* the Civil Procedure Rules 1998, Part 32, requires parties to civil proceedings to serve witness statements on the other parties. These are written statements of the admissible evidence to be given by their non-expert witnesses. Unless the court orders otherwise, witness statements will stand as the evidence in chief of the relevant witnesses, though cross-examination and re-examination will still take place. Where a party is unable to obtain a witness statement the court may, under CPR 32.9, permit the party to serve a witness summary instead. A witness summary is a summary of the evidence which would be in the witness statement or, if this is not known, of the matters about which the party intends to question the witness.]

Calling the maker of a hearsay statement for cross-examination upon it

The effect of s.3 of the Civil Evidence Act 1995 in conjunction with CPR 33.4 is that where a party to civil proceedings intends to adduce a hearsay statement in evidence instead of calling its maker as a witness, another party may, within 14 days of the service of notice of intention to rely upon the hearsay evidence upon him, seek the permission of the court to call the maker and cross-examine him on the hearsay statement as though he had been called by the party who adduced it in evidence. Where the court does give a party permission to call the maker of a hearsay statement tendered by another party for cross-examination and the maker of the hearsay statement fails to attend the proceedings, the court may exclude the hearsay evidence in the exercise of its exclusionary discretion under CPR 32.1 (*Polanski v Conde Nast Publications Ltd* (2004)).

The evidential weight of a hearsay statement

Essentially, s.4 of the Civil Evidence Act 1995 provides that the court, when considering the weight of a hearsay statement (*i.e.* its probative value), may take into account any circumstances from which it is reasonable to draw an inference as to its reliability. In particular, s.4 provides that the court may, for this purpose, consider:

- "whether it would have been reasonable and practicable for the party by whom the evidence was adduced to have produced the maker of the original statement as a witness";

- "whether the original statement was made contemporaneously with the occurrence or existence of the matters stated";
- "whether the evidence involves multiple hearsay";
- "whether any person involved had any motive to conceal or misrepresent matters";
- "whether the original statement was an edited account, or was made in collaboration with another or for a particular purpose";
- "whether the circumstances in which the evidence is adduced as hearsay are such as to suggest an attempt to prevent proper evaluation of its weight."

Competence and compellability

Section 5(1) of the Civil Evidence Act 1995 provides that a hearsay statement is inadmissible in civil proceedings if its maker would not have been a competent witness at the time of its making. Section 5(1) also provides that a hearsay statement is inadmissible in civil proceedings if proved by a statement made by a person who was not a competent witness at the time when he made his statement. The burden of proving that the relevant person was not competent at the relevant time is borne by the party who asserts that this was so (*C v C* (2001)).

[*Note:* the competence of witnesses in civil proceedings was considered in Chapter 2 above.]

Credibility

Section 5(2) of the Civil Evidence Act 1995 provides that, where the maker of a hearsay statement is not called as a witness, evidence is admissible to attack or support his credibility to the extent to which it would have been admissible had he been called and evidence of other inconsistent statements which he has made is admissible to contradict his hearsay evidence. The section makes identical provision concerning the credibility and inconsistent statements of the maker of a statement used to prove a hearsay statement. In either case, however, subject to the exceptions identified in Chapter 5 above, the section effectively upholds the principle that evidence cannot be called in rebuttal of answers to collateral questions by providing that evidence relating to a matter cannot be adduced if it could not have been adduced if the maker of the relevant statement had been called as a witness and had denied the matter when cross-examined.

Where a party to civil proceedings intends to attack the credibility of the maker of a hearsay statement which is to be adduced in evidence by another party without calling the maker, CPR 33.5 requires the former party to notify the latter party of his intention within 14 days of service of a hearsay notice upon him.

Common law exceptions to the hearsay rule preserved in civil proceedings

Section 7(1) of the Civil Evidence Act 1995 abolishes what was formally the most important remaining common law exception to the hearsay rule in civil proceedings, namely, the rule that informal admissions (namely, statements adverse to their maker's interests) made by a party were admissible in evidence against him. Informal admissions are now admissible under s.1 of the 1995 Act and are thus subject to the provisions of ss.2 to 6 of the Act.

Section 7(2) preserves a number of minor common law exceptions to the hearsay rule (for example, the rule that published works (such as dictionaries) concerning public matters are admissible in evidence). Where evidence is admissible under a preserved common law exception to the hearsay rule, the provisions of ss.2 to 6 of the 1995 Act do not apply to it.

Finally, s.7(3) partially preserves a number of common law rules concerning the admissibilitiy of evidence of reputation, though such evidence must now satisfy the requirements of ss.2 to 6 of the 1995 Act.

Proving statements contained in documents

Section 8 of the Civil Evidence Act 1995 provides that, provided that they are admissible in evidence, statements contained in documents may be proved in civil proceedings either by producing the original documents or by producing copies of the documents or of the relevant parts thereof, authenticated in a manner approved by the court. The section also provides that, for this purpose, a copy need not be directly copied from the original document but may be a copy of a copy, it being irrelevant how many levels of copying there are between the original document and the copy. Where an original document is not readily available to a party, the party may be permitted to prove its contents at common law by relying upon the oral evidence of a witness who read the document (*Masquerade Music Ltd v Springsteen* (2001)).

[*Note:* production essentially appears to entail calling a witness to produce a document, though it appears that a document may, alternatively, be proved by other admissible evidence (*Ventouris v Mountain* [1992]). Where a witness is called solely for the purpose of producing a document, the witness need not take the oath (*Perry v Gibson* (1834)).]

Essentially, s.9 of the Civil Evidence Act 1995 provides that it is unnecessary to call witnesses or to adduce other evidence to prove documents which are certified to form part of business or public authority records by officers of the relevant businesses or public authorities. The court may, however, in appropriate circumstances, direct that the provisions of s.9 do not apply to particular documents or types of document.

EXCLUSIONARY DISCRETION

Under CPR 32.1 the civil courts now possess discretion to exclude evidence which would otherwise be admissible. Rule 32.1 entitles the court to: give directions as to the issues in relation to which it requires evidence; give directions as to the nature of the evidence which it requires; give directions as to the way in which evidence is to be placed before it; exclude admissible evidence; and limit cross-examination.

11. CONFESSIONS AND IMPROPERLY OBTAINED EVIDENCE

[*Note:* this chapter is written as though the evidence provisions of the Criminal Justice Act 2003 are already in force. The relevant provisions are due to be brought into force in 2005.]

In this chapter, we will consider both what constitutes a confession and how the courts determine whether confessions are admissible in evidence.

THE MEANING OF "CONFESSION"

Section 82(1) of the Police and Criminal Evidence Act 1984 (PACE) defines a confession as including,

> ". . . any statement wholly or partly adverse to the person who made it, whether made to a person in authority or not and whether made in words or otherwise . . ."

Thus, a statement is a confession if, whether oral, written or made by conduct (*e.g.* by video re-enactment), it is, at least in part, adverse to its maker's interests. For example, if D, being charged with the murder of V by shooting her, admits that he was the only person who was with V at the time of her death but denies shooting her, V's statement is a confession even though it is partly in his favour because, by placing him at the scene of the crime at the time of its commission, it is, in part, adverse to his interests.

DETERMINING THE ADMISSIBILITY OF A CONFESSION: THE *VOIR DIRE*

The statutory provision which regulates the admissibility of confessions is s.76 of PACE (see below). Challenges to the admissibility of confessions are determined "on the *voir dire*" (*i.e.* in a trial within a trial) during which the jury is not present and the judge is not concerned with the truthfulness of the confession. If the confession is not admitted, then the jury are not told of its existence. If the confession is admitted, it is put before the jury but the defence may still try to persuade the jury that it should not be believed (as the jury are concerned with its truthfulness). If the defence do not challenge the admissibility of a confession before it is put before the jury, it appears that its admissibility cannot subsequently be challenged under s.76 (*R. v Sat-Bhambra* (1988)), though the defence may still try to persuade the jury that the confession should not be believed. Moreover, if the defence assert that no confession was ever made there is no need for a *voir dire* as it is for the jury, not the judge, to decide whether this is so (*Ajhoda v The State* (1982)).

Where a *voir dire* is held, the Privy Council stated, in *R. v Wong Kam Ming* (1980), that: the accused cannot be questioned about the truthfulness of his confession during the *voir dire*; statements which he makes during the *voir dire* cannot be made known to the jury; and inconsistencies between the accused's evidence and statements which he made during the *voir dire* cannot be made known to the jury unless his confession is admitted.

Finally, if the admissibility of a confession is challenged under s.76 during summary trial, the magistrates must, similarly, hold a trial within a trial (*R. v Liverpool Juvenile Court* (1988)). During the *voir dire* the magistrates, like the judge in a jury trial, are not concerned with the truthfulness of the confession.

DETERMINING THE ADMISSIBILITY OF A CONFESSION: THE STATUTORY CONDITIONS OF ADMISSIBILITY

A confession is hearsay evidence. However, a confession may be admissible under the hearsay exception provided by s.76 of PACE. The effect of s.128(2) of the Criminal Justice Act 2003 is that where a confession is inadmissible under s.76, it will not be admissible under any other exception to the hearsay rule.

Section 76(1) provides for the admissibility of relevant confessions in the criminal trials of their makers, as evidence against their makers, subject to conditions of admissibility laid down by s.76(2). Section 76(1) and (2) provide as follows:

> "(1) In any [criminal] proceedings a confession made by an accused person may be given in evidence against him in so far as it is relevant to any matter in issue in the proceedings and is not excluded by the court in pursuance of this section.
>
> (2) If, in any proceedings where the prosecution proposes to give in evidence a confession made by an accused person, it is represented to the court that the confession was or may have been obtained—
>
> > (a) by oppression of the person who made it; or
> >
> > (b) in consequence of anything said or done which was likely, in the circumstances existing at the time, to render unreliable any confession which might be made by him in consequence thereof, the court shall not allow the confession to be given in evidence against him except in so far as the prosecution proves to the court beyond reasonable doubt that the confession (notwithstanding that it may be true) was not obtained as aforesaid."

Thus, if the defence suggest (or the court of its own motion raises the issue—s.76(3)) that the means by which, or circumstances in which, a confession was obtained fall within paragraphs (a) or (b) of s.76(2), the confession will only be admissible if the prosecution can prove beyond a reasonable doubt that the confession was not obtained in either of the ways set out in those paragraphs. Further, s.76(2) makes clear, and the court has confirmed this in *R. v Crampton* (1991), that whether the confession is true or not is not a relevant consideration in assessing its admissibility.

[*Note:* students will inevitably be required to demonstrate a high degree of familiarity with s.76(2) in answering examination questions on confessions. Problem questions on confessions will invariably contain examples of conduct, usually on the part of police officers, which may amount to oppression or give rise to unreliability. It is, therefore, extremely important both to know what is meant by oppression and unreliability and to appreciate when oppression and unreliability may render a confession inadmissible.]

Oppression (section 76(2)(a))

In order to establish that a confession was not "obtained by oppression", the prosecution must prove, to the criminal stand-ard of proof, **either** that the accused did not confess in conse-quence of the oppression to which he was subjected **or** that he was not subjected to oppression.

When is a confession "obtained" by oppression? It appears from the wording of s.76(2)(a) that if the prosecution can prove that the accused did not confess because he was oppressed but for some other reason, then the confession is not rendered inadmissible by paragraph (a). In determining whether the oppression to which the accused was subjected may have "produced" the accused's confession, it seems that the court will take relevant aspects of his personality into account to decide whether these render it more or less likely that he will "crack" under pressure. Thus, the courts have recognised that conduct which might "persuade" a person of very low intelligence to confess might not have this effect when directed at someone who is intelligent and sophisticated (respectively, *R. v Miller, R. v Parris, R. v Abdullahi* (1992) and *R. v Seelig* (1992)).

The nature of oppression A confession is not rendered inadmissible by s.76(2) if the prosecution can prove that the conduct to which the accused was subjected did not amount to oppression. Section 76(8) provides that oppression includes:

"... torture, inhuman or degrading treatment, and the use or threat of violence (whether or not amounting to torture)."

A more comprehensive definition was adopted in *R. v Fulling* (1987) by Lord Lane C.J. who stated that oppression should be given its dictionary meaning which, according to the Oxford English Dictionary, is the;

"Exercise of authority or power in a burdensome, harsh or wrong-ful manner; unjust or cruel treatment of subjects, inferiors etc; the imposition of unreasonable or unjust burdens."

His Lordship was of the view that oppression in this sense would almost certainly involve improper conduct by persons interviewing the accused.

Examples of conduct on the part of police officers which appears potentially capable of giving rise to oppression include breaches of the requirements of PACE or of the Codes of Practice made under PACE and "heavy handed" questioning or distortion of evidence on the part of interviewing officers. For example, it appears that failure to provide access to a solicitor as required by s.58 of PACE may, if a consequence of bad faith, amount to oppression (*R. v Alladice* (1988)). Similarly, where interviewing officers persistently shouted allegations at the accused even though he had consistently denied his guilt several hundred times over a number of days, their conduct was held to amount to oppression (*R. v Miller, R. v Parris, R. v Abdullahi*). Again, where interviewing officers deliberately set out to persuade the accused that the case against him is stronger than, in fact, it is, it appears that their conduct may amount to oppression (*R. v Beales* (1991)).

Conversely, the mere fact that conduct is improper does not, in itself, mean that the conduct is oppressive if the degree of impropriety is trivial (*R. v Emmerson* (1990) and *R. v Parker* (1995)).

Unreliability (section 76(2)(b))

In order to establish that a confession was not "obtained in consequence of anything said or done which was likely, in the circumstances existing at the time, to render unreliable any confession which [the accused] might [have made] in consequence [of the thing said or done]", the prosecution must prove, to the criminal standard of proof, either that the accused did not confess in consequence of the thing said or done, or that the thing said or done was not likely to have rendered unreliable any confession made by him in consequence of the thing said or done, in the circumstances in which he did confess.

When is a confession "obtained" in consequence of the thing said or done? It appears from the wording of s.76(2)(b) that if the prosecution can prove that the accused did not confess because the thing was said or done but for some other reason, then the confession is not rendered inadmissible by paragraph (b). In determining whether the thing said or done may have "produced" the accused's confession, it seems that the court will take relevant aspects of his personality into account. Such factors may sometimes make it more likely that the accused confessed in response to the thing said or done but sometimes may have the opposite effect. For example, failure to provide access to a solicitor as required by s.58 of PACE might be a factor which could lead a person of low intelligence who knows little about the criminal process to confess, but may well be less likely to have this effect upon a person who has the ability to cope with an "interview situation" and is aware of his legal rights (see, respectively, *R. v Harvey* (1988) and *R. v Alladice*).

What types of "things" and "circumstances" are capable of producing unreliability? A confession is not rendered inadmissible by s.76(2)(b) if the prosecution can prove that the thing said or done was not likely to have rendered unreliable any confession made by the accused in consequence of the thing said or done in the circumstances in which he did confess.

In contrast with oppression, improper conduct does not form an essential pre-requisite of unreliability (*R. v Fulling*). Further, whether or not the accused's confession is or is not likely to be unreliable is not the issue before the court, the court being concerned with the likely reliability of any confession which he might have made in the circumstances, in consequence of the thing said or done (*R. v Crampton* (1991)).

The court, when deciding whether to exclude a confession under s.76(2)(b), must consider three issues:

(1) Whether anything relevant was said or done;

(2) The nature of the circumstances existing at the time when the thing was said or done;

(3) Whether in those circumstances, the thing said or done was likely to render any confession which the accused might have made in consequence of the thing said or done unreliable.

Examples of things said or done which might, in appropriate circumstances, be relevant to the operation of paragraph (a) are: breaches of requirements laid down by PACE or by the Codes of Practice made under PACE (*R. v Trussler* (1988)); inducements to confess in the form of offers of favourable treatment (*R. v Mathias* (1989)); or statements to the effect that close friends or relatives of the accused are implicated in the commission of the crime under investigation (*R. v Harvey*).

The thing said or done must be said or done by someone other than the accused himself (*R. v Goldenberg* (1988) and *R. v Wahab* (2003)). Thus, if the accused confesses in the hope that he will be released on bail and, consequently, will be able to obtain alcohol or drugs in order to satisfy his craving, this will not be sufficient to render his confession inadmissible under paragraph (b) unless this hope has been created or fostered by the words or conduct of others.

The circumstances existing at the time when the "thing" was said or done may make it more or less likely that a consequent confession would be unreliable. For example, the absence of a legal adviser may result in the accused attaching more weight to an inducement to confess than he would have done had he received proper legal advice before confessing (*R. v Mathias*). Similarly, the mental illness and low intelligence of the accused may increase the likelihood that, upon hearing that her lover has confessed to a crime, she would confess in order to protect her (*R. v Harvey*).

Finally, the fact that circumstances which make it more likely that a confession made by the accused will be unreliable are unknown to the interviewing officers at the time when they say or do the relevant thing does not prevent the court from taking account of those circumstances when determining the admissibility of the accused's confession under paragraph (b). Thus, for example, the fact that the officers are not aware of the accused's low mental age would not prevent the court from considering this factor when considering whether things said or done by the officers were likely to have rendered unreliable a consequent confession by him (*R. v Everett* (1988)).

Judicial discretion to refuse to permit the prosecution to adduce a confession in evidence

[*Note:* in answering exam questions on confessions, students will normally be required not only to consider whether a confession is rendered inadmissible by s.76(2) but will also be required to consider whether, upon the assumption that the operation of s.76(2) does not render the confession inadmissible, the court should exclude the confession in the exercise of its exclusionary discretion.]

Where the operation of s.76(2) of PACE does not render a confession inadmissible as prosecution evidence, the court (trial judge or magistrates) may permit the prosecution to adduce the confession in evidence, but is not obliged to do so. Rather, the court possesses discretion to refuse to permit the prosecution to adduce a confession in evidence.

The basis of this exclusionary discretion (which extends to all forms of prosecution evidence, not just to confessions) is s.8 of PACE, which provides that the court may refuse to allow the prosecution to adduce evidence,

> ". . . if it appears to the court that having regard to all the circumstances, including the circumstances in which the evidence was obtained, the admission of the evidence would have such an adverse effect on the fairness of the proceedings that the court ought not to admit it.".

Whilst, in practice, the courts usually make use of s.78 when refusing to admit confession evidence in the exercise of their discretion, the extent of their discretion is not limited to circumstances encompassed by s.78. Rather, s.82(3) preserves the discretion to exclude prosecution evidence which the criminal courts possessed prior to the enactment of PACE.

Essentially, the effect of these two provisions of PACE, when viewed together, appears to be that the criminal courts are prepared to exclude confessions in the exercise of their discretion for the following reasons, though it is not suggested that this list is exhaustive.

   (a) *Where there has been a breach of requirement laid down either by PACE or by one of the Codes of Practice made under PACE:* It appears that the exercise of exclusionary discretion is justified where the breach is "significant and substantial", though the fact that a breach is significant and substantial does not automatically require the exclusion of a confession in every case (*R. v Walsh* (1989)).

Thus, it may not be appropriate to exclude a confession in respect of a breach which is trivial (such as not showing the accused the record of his interview *R. v Matthews* (1989)) or which has insignificant practical consequences. For example, the court may decline to exercise its discretion where, although there has been a failure to provide the accused with a solicitor as requested, the court is satisfied that this has not adversely affected the accused's interests because he has the ability to cope with an "interview situation" and is aware of his legal rights (*R. v Alladice*).

In contrast, if a breach has significant practical consequences, the exercise of exclusionary discretion may well be appropriate. Thus, if the court is of the opinion that the accused would probably not have confessed had he received legal advice as requested, the court is likely to exercise its exclusionary discretion (*R. v Samuel* (1988)).

Further, even where a breach does not have significant practical consequences, bad faith on the part of the interviewer may persuade the court to exercise its discretion. Thus, where the court is satisfied that failure to provide the accused with a solicitor did not adversely affect his interests, the court may still be prepared to exercise its exclusionary discretion if the failure to comply with the accused's request amounted to a deliberate decision not to comply with the requirements of PACE (*R. v Alladice*).

(b) *Where a confession has been obtained by unfair means:* In *R. v Mason* (1987) police officers told the accused and his solicitor that the accused's fingerprints had been found at the scene of the crime (arson) on a bottle containing inflammable liquid. This was a deliberate lie but it persuaded the accused's solicitor to advise him to answer police questions and explain his involvement in the offence with the result that he confessed. The Court of Appeal held that the trial judge should have excluded the confession in the exercise of his discretion.

(c) *Where the probative value of the confession is outweighed by its prejudicial effect:* If the judge feels that the evidential value of a confession is small (perhaps, for example, because of the mental illness of the accused at the time when he made it), he may be prepared to exercise his exclusionary discretion so as to prevent the jury being prejudiced by knowledge of the confession (*R. v Miller* (1986)).

What if a first confession is excluded but the accused has confessed at a later interview which was properly conducted? Sometimes, following the making of a confession which the court either cannot admit, due to the operation of s.76(2), or will not admit in the exercise of its discretion, it may be that the accused was interviewed again, and made a further confession. Where this is the case, even if nothing happened in the course of the second interview which would require or justify exclusion of the confession, the courts have held that the conduct which required or justified exclusion of the first confession may remain an operative factor which either requires the exclusion of the second on grounds of oppression or unreliability or justifies its exclusion in the exercise of judicial discretion (see, respectively, *R. v Ismail* (1991); *R. v McGovern* (1991); and *R. v Gillard and Barrett* (1991)).

Is an accused's confession admissible evidence for the prosecution against his co-accused? Usually, a confession is only admissible in evidence for the prosecution against the person who made it. It cannot be used against a co-accused whom it implicates as this would infringe the hearsay rule, the hearsay exception contained in s.76 of PACE only permitting the admission of a confession as evidence against its maker. However, if an accused, whilst being interviewed, accepts that a confession, implicating him, which was made by a co-accused is true, the confession also becomes his confession and may be used against him (*R. v Christie* (1914)).

Is an accused's confession admissible in evidence for a co-accused? Section 76A of PACE 1984 provides that an accused's confession is admissible in evidence for a co-accused in so far as it is relevant to a matter in issue and is not excluded under s.76A. The section applies the same test for admissibility of a confession adduced by a co-accused as that for a confession adduced by the prosecution, *i.e.* it will be inadmissible if it was, or may have been, obtained by oppression or in consequence of anything said or done which was likely, in the circumstances existing at the time, to render unreliable any confession which might be made by him in consequence thereof. However, there is a difference in the standard of proof required: where the co-accused seeks to prove that the confession was not obtained in either of these ways, he only has to satisfy the court of this on the **balance of probabilities** (whereas the standard of proof for the prosecution is proof beyond reasonable doubt).

Admissibility of facts discovered as a result of a confession Sometimes when an accused makes a confession, he also provides information as to the where-abouts of items connected with the offence (*e.g.* the murder weapon) which the prosecution may later wish to adduce in evidence against him. The admissibility and evidential significance of such evidence depends, to some extent, upon the admissibility of the confession itself.

(a) *Where the confession is admissible:* Evidence of the discovery of relevant items in consequence of the confession is also admissible, the prosecution being entitled to reveal to the jury how the items were discovered.

(b) *Where the confession is excluded under s.76 of PACE:* The effect of s.76(4) is that the fact that the items have been discovered in a particular location is still admissible. The effect of ss.76(5) and 76(6) is, however, that the prosecution cannot reveal to the jury how the items were discovered.

For example, assume that D confesses to burglary. As a result, stolen property is found in his car. The confession is excluded under s.76. The fact that the property was found in his car is admissible but the prosecution may not refer to the confession. Thus, they cannot reveal to the jury that the police searched D's car because D had told them when he confessed that the stolen property could be found there.

In this example, the fact that the property was found in D's car is cogent evidence against him even though the confession is inadmissible. Suppose, however, that D had informed the police that he had stolen the property and left it in a stolen car. In this case, if D's confession was inadmissible and the stolen car could not be linked to D in some other way, the fact that the property was discovered in the stolen car would appear to be of limited evidential significance.

(c) *Where the confession is excluded in the exercise of the common law or statutory discretion:* Section 76(4) provides that it only applies where a confession is "excluded in pursuance of" s.76. It does not apply where, in the exercise of its discretion, the court refuses to allow the prosecution to adduce a confession in evidence. It appears, however, that in such circumstances, common law principles, the effect of which are similar to that of s.76(4), will probably apply. (*R. v Warickshall* (1783) provides an example of the application of these common law principles prior to the enactment of PACE).

Like s.76(4), s.76(5) and (6) only apply where a confession is "excluded in pursuance of" s.76. The common law position concerning the extent to which the prosecution may reveal to the jury how the items were discovered where the court excludes a confession in the exercise of its discretion is unclear.

Excluded confessions as evidence of their makers' manner of communication

Section 76(4) also provides that:

> "The fact that a confession is wholly or partly excluded in pursuance of this section shall not affect the admissibility in evidence—
> (b) where the confession is relevant as showing that the accused speaks, writes or expresses himself in a particular way, of so much of the confession as is necessary to show that he does so."

When a confession is excluded under s.76 part or all of it may still be admissible to prove that its maker "speaks, writes or expresses himself in a particular way", where this is relevant to an issue before the court (PACE s.76(4)(b)). Only so much of the confession as is required to prove the accused's manner of communication is admissible.

Confessions made by unaccompanied mentally handicapped persons

Where a confession made by a mentally handicapped person in the absence of an independent person is admitted in evidence against him and the prosecution case is based wholly or substantially upon the confession, s.77 of PACE applies. The effect of s.77 is, essentially, that the trial judge must explain to the jury (or that the magistrates must be aware) that, in the circumstances, they must exercise especial caution prior to convicting the accused.

This requirement does not apply if an independent person (*i.e.* a person independent of the police force) was present when the accused confessed.

[*Note:* in many cases in which a mentally handicapped person confesses in the absence of an independent person, s.77 will be irrelevant in practice as the confession will be excluded under s.76 or in the exercise of judicial discretion. The provision of a warning under s.77 does not render admissible a confession which otherwise would be excluded (*R. v Moss* (1990).]

Judicial discretion to exclude illegally, unfairly or improperly obtained prosecution evidence other than confessions

As has already been seen in the course of this chapter, the admissibility of confessions for the prosecution in criminal proceedings is now governed by s.76 of the Police and Criminal Evidence Act 1984. The fact that prosecution evidence other than a confession was obtained illegally, unfairly or improperly does not render the evidence inadmissible at common law (*R. v Sang* (1980)) and there is no statutory provision equivalent to s.76 of the 1984 Act which might render such evidence admissible. Rather, where such evidence is relevant to an issue in criminal proceedings it will be admissible for the prosecution unless the court excludes it in the exercise of its exclusionary discretion under s.78 of the 1984 Act (or, much less likely, in the exercise of its common law exclusionary discretion). Thus, for example, where the defence alleges that evidence was obtained from the accused by an undercover police officer acting as an agent provocateur (see, for example, *R. v Smurthwaite* (1994)) or in consequence of breaches of requirements imposed by Code D (concerning the conduct of identification parades, etc.) (*R. v Quinn* (1990)), the evidence will only be excluded if the judge, in the exercise of his exclusionary discretion, decides that the admission of the evidence would, in the circumstances, have such an adverse effect on the fairness of the proceedings that it ought not to be admitted.

In relation to breaches of requirements of the Police and Criminal Evidence Act 1984 or of the Codes of Practice, exclusion under s.78 of the 1984 Act is likely where the breach is significant or substantial or in bad faith (*R. v Walsh*). Where the breach is not significant, substantial or deliberate and the evidence is admitted, an appropriate direction to the jury may be required (*R. v Quinn*).

[*Note:* in relation to entrapment the grant of a stay of proceedings will normally be the appropriate remedy and if the issue of entrapment arises in the context of the exercise of the s.78 discretion the evidence should be excluded either if there has been procedural unfairness or if condoning the police conduct would bring the administration of justice into disrepute (*R. v Loosely* (2001)).]

The admission for the prosecution in criminal proceedings of illegally, improperly or unfairly obtained evidence (*e.g.* evidence obtained by entrapment) may give rise to a violation of Art.6 of the European Convention on Human Rights (*Teixera de Castro v Portugal* (1999)). It is submitted, however, that where a criminal court, having properly considered the exercise of the s.78 exclusionary discretion and having properly taken into account any relevant human rights arguments, determines that evidence such as evidence obtained by entrapment (*Nottingham City Council v Amin* (2000)) or evidence obtained in consequence of violation of Art.8 of the Convention (*Khan v UK* (1997)) should be admitted, the admission of such evidence will be unlikely to give rise to a violation of Art.6.

12. STATUTORY EXCEPTIONS TO THE HEARSAY RULE IN CRIMINAL PROCEEDINGS (OTHER THAN CONFESSIONS)

[*Note:* this chapter is written as though the evidence provisions of the Criminal Justice Act 2003 are already in force. The relevant provisions are due to be brought into force in 2005. Applicable Rules of Court will be contained in the new Criminal Procedure Rules 2005.]

This chapter deals with the statutory exceptions to the hearsay rule (other than confessions) which permit the admission of hearsay evidence. There are statutory exceptions other than those examined in this chapter. However, only those exceptions which will feature most commonly in examination questions are considered here, *i.e.* those under the Criminal Justice Act 2003. These provisions are exceptions to the hearsay rule only. Consequently, they do not render admissible statements which are inadmissible because they fall within another exclusionary rule of evidence in addition to the hearsay rule.

SITUATIONS WHERE A WITNESS IS UNAVAILABLE—SECTION 116

Section 116 permits the admission of oral or documentary hearsay provided the following conditions are satisfied:

(1) The oral evidence of the maker of the statement would be admissible as evidence of the relevant matter.

Thus, for example, if the maker could not have given direct oral testimony of the facts because his oral evidence would itself have been hearsay, the statement will be inadmissible under s.116.

(2) The maker of the statement is identified to the court's satisfaction.

(3) One of the conditions contained in s.116 for not calling the maker of the statement must be satisfied. The conditions are that the maker:
  (i) is dead OR
  (ii) is unfit to be a witness by reason of his bodily or mental condition OR
  (iii) is outside the United Kingdom and it is not reasonably practicable to secure his attendance OR
  (iv) cannot be found, all reasonable steps having been taken to find him OR
  (v) does not give oral evidence (or does not continue to give evidence) either at all or in connection with the relevant matter through fear and the court grants leave for the statement to be admitted in evidence.

The interpretation of the section 116 conditions

Conditions (i)–(iv) were also statutory reasons for not calling the maker of a hearsay statement under the equivalent provision, s.23 of the Criminal Justice Act 1988, which was repealed by the

Criminal Justice Act 2003. It is, therefore, likely that a similar interpretation will be given by the courts to the conditions as was given to the statutory reasons. Under the CJA 1988, the statutory reasons were interpreted as follows:

(1) The reason that the witness "is outside the UK . . ." could not be used in respect of a witness who resided in a foreign embassy within the United Kingdom (see *Carmenza Jiminez-Paez* (1994)).

(2) With regard to the practicability of securing the attendance of a witness who was outside the United Kingdom, this was determined at the date of the application to admit the witness's statement (*R. v French and Gowhar* (1993)), and by taking into account: (i) the importance of the witness's evidence and whether or not it was prejudicial; (ii) the issues of cost and inconvenience; and (iii) the arguments raised as to why attendance was not reasonably practicable (*R. v Castillo* (1996)).

With regard to condition (v), *i.e.* that the witness is unavailable through fear, the term "fear" is to be widely construed and includes fear of the death or injury of another person and fear of financial loss. Where a party wishes to rely on this condition they must obtain the leave of the court to admit the statement. Leave may be given only if the court considers that the statement ought to be admitted in the interests of justice. In applying the interests of justice test, the court is specifically directed to consider:

(a) The contents of the statement;

(b) The risk that its admission or exclusion will result in unfairness to any party to the proceedings (and in particular to how difficult it will be to challenge the statement if the maker of the hearsay statement does not give oral evidence);

(c) If appropriate, the fact that a special measures direction under YJCEA 1999, s.19 (see Chapter 5) could be made in relation to the maker of the hearsay statement; and

(d) Any other relevant circumstances.

[*Note:* where one of the five conditions is in fact satisfied, it will be treated as not being satisfied if it is shown that the relevant circumstances were caused by the party who wishes to rely on the hearsay statement or by someone acting on his behalf, with the aim of preventing the maker of the hearsay statement from testifying.]

BUSINESS AND OTHER DOCUMENTS—SECTION 117

Section 117 permits the admission of a hearsay statement provided the following conditions are satisfied:

(1) The statement must be contained in a document.
(2) Oral evidence would be admissible as evidence of the relevant matter.
(3) The document or the part containing the statement was created or received by a person in the course of a trade, business, profession or other occupation, or as the holder of a paid or unpaid office.

   Who must act in the course of a trade, business profession, etc? No obligation is imposed on the supplier of the information to have acted in the course of his trade, business or profession. Only the person who created or received the document must have done so in such capacity. Where, however, the information contained in the document passes through intermediaries before reaching the person who creates or receives the document, the intermediaries must also receive the information in the course of a trade, business, profession, etc.

(4) The information contained in the document was supplied by a person who had, or may reasonably be supposed to have had, personal knowledge of the matters dealt with.
(5) A fifth requirement is imposed if the statement was prepared for the purposes of pending or contemplated criminal proceedings or for the purposes of a criminal investigation. Section 117(4) provides that a documentary statement prepared for any of the aforementioned reasons will not be admissible under s.117 unless:

   (a) There is a s.116 condition for not calling supplier of the information; or
   (b) The reason the supplier of the information is not called is that he cannot reasonably be expected (having regard to the time which has elapsed since he made the statement and to all the circumstances) to have any recollection of the matters dealt with in his statement.

MULTIPLE HEARSAY—SECTION 121

Section 121 imposes an additional requirement for the admissibility of multiple hearsay. Multiple hearsay is where a statement which is itself hearsay is used to prove that another hearsay statement was made. For example, W makes a statement to X who repeats it to Y. Z overhears X repeating the statement to Y. The repetition of the statement in court by Y or Z would be multiple hearsay. Such a hearsay statement will only be admissible if one of the following conditions is satisfied:

(a) Either of the statements is admissible under s.117, 119 (inconsistent statements) or 120 (previous statements);
(b) All the parties agree to its admission; or
(c) The value of the evidence, taking into account how reliable the statements appear to be, is so high that the interests of justice require the later statement to be admissible for the purpose of proving the earlier statement.

INCLUSIONARY DISCRETION—SECTION 114(d)

The court may grant leave to admit an otherwise inadmissible hearsay statement where satisfied that it is in the interests of justice to do so. In determining whether leave is in the interests of justice, the court is required to consider the following factors (as well as any others it considers relevant):

(a) Assuming the statement to be true, the probative value of the statement in relation to an issue in the proceedings, or how valuable it is for the understanding of other evidence in the case;
(b) Any other evidence which has been, or can be, given on the relevant issue or other evidence in the case;
(c) The importance of the relevant issue or other evidence in the case in the context of the case as a whole;
(d) The circumstances in which the statement was made;
(e) The reliability of the maker of the statement;
(f) The reliability of the evidence of the making of the statement;
(g) Whether oral evidence of the relevant issue can be given and, if not, why not;
(h) The level of difficulty involved in challenging the statement;

(i) The extent to which that difficulty would be likely to prejudice the party facing it.

Are there any human rights implications of admitting hearsay evidence? See Chapter 9.

THE COURT'S POWERS TO EXCLUDE HEARSAY STATEMENTS WHICH ARE OTHERWISE ADMISSIBLE

The courts have three separate powers to exclude otherwise admissible hearsay evidence:

(1) Section 117(6)–(7) provides the court with a discretion to exclude hearsay evidence adduced by either the prosecution or the defence under s.117 on the grounds that the statement's reliability as evidence of the relevant matter is doubtful in view of:
  (a) Its contents; or
  (b) The source of the information contained in it; or
  (c) The way in which or the circumstances in which the information was supplied or received; or
  (d) The way in which or the circumstances in which the document concerned was created or received.

(2) The court's common law exclusionary discretion to exclude evidence where its prejudicial effect outweighs its probative value and its discretion under s.78 of PACE may be used to exclude hearsay statements which the prosecution seek to adduce.

(3) The court has a discretion under s.126 to exclude hearsay evidence adduced by either the prosecution or the defence under s.116 or 117 where satisfied that the case for excluding the statement, taking into account the danger that its admission would result in undue waste of time, substantially outweighs the case for admitting it, taking into account the value of the evidence.

CAPABILITY OF THE MAKER/SUPPLIER, ETC.—SECTION 123

Section 123 provides that a hearsay statement will not be admissible under s.116, 119 or 120 if it was made by a person who lacked the required capability (competence) at the time the statement was made. Similarly, a hearsay statement will not be admissible under s.117 if the supplier or receiver of the information or the creator or receiver of the document (and any intermediaries) lacked the required capability (or, where that person cannot be identified, cannot reasonably be assumed to have the required capability) at the time the information was supplied/received or the document was created/received.

A person will have the required capability if he is capable of understanding questions put to him about the matters contained in the hearsay statement and of giving answers to those questions which can be understood.

Where the issue of the capability of a person is raised, the party seeking to adduce the statement bears the burden of proving that person's capability on the balance of probabilities. Proceedings to determine the issue will take place in the absence of the jury and expert evidence and evidence from a person to whom the statement was made may be received for the purpose of determining the issue.

CREDIBILITY—SECTION 124

Section 124 provides that where the maker of a hearsay statement does not testify, the following evidence is admissible to attack his credibility:

(a) Evidence which would have been admissible had he testified;
(b) With leave, evidence of a collateral matter;
(c) Evidence of any other inconsistent statements in order to show that the maker has contradicted himself.

Where a statement is admitted under s.117, s.124 applies also to the supplier or receiver of the information or the creator or receiver of the document and to any intermediaries.

If evidence of credibility is adduced under s.124, the court may allow a party to adduce evidence to deny or answer the allegation.

PROOF OF STATEMENTS IN DOCUMENTS—SECTION 133

Section 133 provides that a statement contained in a document which is admissible in criminal proceedings may be proved by the production of the document or a copy thereof authenticated in a manner approved by the court.

STOPPING THE CASE WHERE EVIDENCE IS UNCONVINCING —SECTION 125

Section 125 applies to jury trials only. It provides that the trial judge may direct an acquittal or order a retrial where, at any time following the conclusion of the case for the prosecution, he is satisfied that the case against the defendant is based wholly or partly on a hearsay statement which is so unconvincing that, considering its importance to the prosecution's case, the conviction would be unsafe.

13. EVIDENCE OF CHARACTER

[*Note:* this chapter is written as though the evidence provisions of the Criminal Justice Act 2003 are already in force. The relevant provisions are due to be brought into force in 2005. Applicable Rules of Court will be contained in the new Criminal Procedure Rules 2005.]

In this chapter, we will consider: the nature of character evidence; the extent to which the accused in a criminal trial can adduce evidence of his good character and the relevance and effect of such evidence; the circumstances in which the accused may be cross-examined about his bad character and the purpose of such cross-examination; and the extent to which evidence of the bad character of someone other than the accused may be adduced. Finally, the admissibility of evidence of character in civil proceedings as "similar fact evidence" will briefly be considered.

WHAT IS "EVIDENCE OF CHARACTER?"

The term "character", when considered in the context of the Law of Evidence, encompasses: evidence that a person is generally disposed to act in a particular way; evidence of specific instances in which a person acted in a particular way; and evidence as to a person's general reputation in his community. Evidence of character may be of good character (examples being that the witness has no previous convictions, is an upstanding member of the community, attends church regularly or contributes to several local charities) or of bad character (for example, he has several previous convictions or has been charged with a criminal offence).

The three most important issues to consider are admissibility, effect and relevance. The rules relating to the admissibility, effect and relevance of character evidence of the accused depend upon whether the accused chooses to testify or not, whether the evidence is of good or bad character and which party to the proceedings wishes to adduce the evidence.

EVIDENCE OF THE ACCUSED'S GOOD CHARACTER

Admissibility of evidence of good character A restrictive approach to the admissibility of evidence of the accused's good character was adopted in the leading case of *R. v Rowton* (1865). The court held that only evidence of the accused's general reputation in the community would be admissible. Thus, an accused could not call witnesses to testify or, through his counsel, cross-examine prosecution witnesses, regarding specific examples of his good deeds or their favourable opinion of him. *Rowton* has never been overruled but has been applied flexibly by the courts. See, for example, *R. v Redgrave* (1981) in which the accused was charged with importuning for immoral purposes. Although the accused was not permitted to adduce photographs of himself with women and love letters in support of his contention that he was heterosexual, the Court of Appeal stated that he might, at the court's discretion, have been allowed to adduce evidence to show that he had a normal sexual relationship with his female partner.

Relevance of evidence of good character This depends on whether or not the accused chooses to testify:

The accused chooses not to testify

Evidence of the accused's good character is relevant to his guilt, *i.e.* to suggest to the court that, as a person of good character, he is unlikely to have committed the offence with which he is charged. Further, where the accused chooses not to testify but wishes to rely on exculpatory pre-trial answers or statements, he is also entitled to a direction on the relevance of his good character to the credibility of such statements (*R. v Vye* (1993)).

The accused testifies

Evidence of the good character of the accused who chooses to testify is relevant to both credit (*i.e.* because he is of good character he is more likely to be speaking the truth than a person of bad character) and guilt (*i.e.* because he is of good character he is less likely to have committed the offence).

An accused who is of good character is entitled to a direction by the judge on the relevance of his good character even if he is jointly charged with an accused who is of bad character (*R. v Vye*).

The exclusionary discretion

The trial judge retains a discretion not to give the direction on the relevance of the accused's good character where he is satisfied that it would be an "insult to common sense" to do so, for example, where the accused has no previous convictions but it has been shown that he has engaged in serious criminal behaviour similar to the offence with which he is charged (*R. v Aziz* (1995)) or, in certain circumstances, where he has previously received a caution for a relevant offence (*R. v Scott* (2000)).

EVIDENCE OF THE ACCUSED'S BAD CHARACTER

The Criminal Justice Act 2003 governs the admissibility of evidence of the accused's bad character.

What is evidence of bad character? This is defined by s.98 as evidence of, or of a disposition towards, misconduct other than evidence which has to do with the alleged facts of the offence with which the accused is charged (*i.e.* evidence of the facts of offence X will not be admissible as evidence of bad character when the court is determining whether the accused committed offence X), or is evidence of misconduct in connection with the investigation or prosecution of that offence. Misconduct is defined in s.112 as the commission of an offence or other reprehensible behaviour. The Explanatory Notes to the statute suggest that this is intended to be a broad definition covering evidence that shows that a person has committed (or is disposed to commit) an offence or has acted (or is disposed to act) in a reprehensible way, as well as evidence from which this might be inferred. The definition is, therefore, intended to include evidence such as previous convictions, as well as evidence on charges being tried concurrently, and evidence relating to offences for which a person has been charged, where the charge is not prosecuted, or for which the person was subsequently acquitted but the prosecution dispute the acquittal (reflecting the common law position in *R. v Z* (2000)).

Section 112(2) provides that where the accused is charged with two or more offences in the same proceedings (though not in relation to s.101(3), discussed below) each offence is treated as if it was charged in separate proceedings. Thus, in the situation where there is a multi count indictment, although evidence which has to do with the alleged facts of an offence with which the accused is charged is not evidence of his bad character, evidence of the facts of that offence will amount to evidence of bad character when the court is considering whether it is admissible in relation to one or more of the other offences with which he is charged. This is so because such evidence will not have to do with the alleged facts of the other offences.

When is evidence of the bad character of the accused admissible?   Section 101 sets out the gateways through which this evidence can be admitted. It provides that evidence of the accused's bad character is admissible if:

(a) All the parties agree to its admission; or
(b) The evidence is adduced by the accused himself or is given in answer to a question asked by him (or his counsel) in cross-examination and intended to elicit it; or
(c) It is important explanatory evidence; or
(d) It is relevant to an important matter in issue between the accused and the prosecution; or
(e) It has substantial probative value in relation to an important matter in issue between the accused and a co-accused; or
(f) It is evidence to correct a false impression given by the accused; or
(g) The accused has made an attack on another person's character.

(a) All the parties agree to its admission

This is self-explanatory.

(b) The evidence is adduced by the accused himself or is given in answer to a question asked by him in cross-examination and intended to elicit it.

Why might an accused adduce evidence of his own bad character?   It may sometimes be good tactics for the accused to testify in chief as to his bad character where he knows that his bad character may become admissible for the prosecution or a co-accused. This is because the jury may look more favourably on an accused who volunteers such evidence and it may be possible for defence counsel to present the evidence in a more positive light.

(c) Important explanatory evidence

This is evidence without which the court would find it impossible or difficult to understand other evidence in the case and which has substantial value for understanding the case as a whole.

(d) Evidence relevant to an important matter in issue between the accused and the prosecution

The prosecution may adduce evidence of the accused's bad character if it is relevant to an important matter at issue between them and the accused.

What is an "important matter in issue"? This is one which has substantial importance in the context of the case as a whole. Examples of such evidence might be that which helps the prosecution to prove the accused's guilt of the offence by establishing his involvement or *mens rea* or by rebutting his explanation of his conduct or evidence to prove that an offence was actually committed.

Can evidence that the accused has a mere propensity to commit offences of the type alleged be admitted? Such evidence can be admitted under s.103(c) unless it makes it no more likely that the accused is guilty. Thus, for example, where there is no dispute about the facts of the case and the question is whether those facts constitute the offence, evidence of propensity would be inadmissible.

Further, evidence relating to the accused's propensity to be untruthful may also be admitted under this provision unless it is not suggested that his case is untruthful.

Propensity may be established by evidence that the accused has been convicted of an offence of the same description or category as the one with which he is charged unless the court is satisfied that due to the length of time since the previous conviction, or for any other reason, that would be unjust. An offence is of the same description if it is the same offence as that charged, *e.g.* a previous conviction for assault where the accused is charged with assault. An offence will be of the same category as another if they both fall within a category drawn up by the Secretary of State in secondary legislation.

Exclusionary Duty Where the evidence of the accused's bad character is admissible under this provision, the accused can apply to have it excluded. The judge must exclude if it would have such an adverse effect on the fairness of the trial that it ought to be excluded (s.101(3)). The test is to be applied as the courts do under s.78 under which the judge assesses the probative value of the evidence to an issue in the case and the prejudicial effect of admitting it in determining whether it would be unfair to admit the evidence. In determining whether to exclude under this provision, the court is specifically directed to take account of the amount of time that has elapsed between the previous events and the current charge.

(e) The evidence has substantial probative value in relation to an important matter in issue between the accused and a co-accused

Only the co-accused may adduce evidence of the accused's bad character under this provision and, once it is satisfied, there is no discretion to exclude the evidence. Evidence of bad character is admissible for a co-accused if it has substantial probative value in relation to an important issue in the case (it helps to prove that issue). Thus, evidence that has only marginal or trivial value would not be admissible, nor would it be admissible if the issue it related to were marginal or trivial in the case as a whole. A co-accused may wish to adduce evidence of the accused's bad character if his defence is, for example, that it was the accused, rather than himself, who was responsible for the offence.

Section 104 restricts the admissibility of evidence of an accused's bad character which merely shows a propensity to be untruthful to circumstances in which the accused has undermined the co-accused's defence.

(f) Evidence to correct a false impression

Only the prosecution may adduce evidence of the accused's bad character under this provision. To apply, the accused must have been responsible for an assertion which gives a false or misleading impression about himself. This might be done expressly, for example, by falsely asserting he is of good character or impliedly, for example, by adducing evidence of his conduct that implies his character is better than it actually is. It may also be done by his conduct in court, such as his appearance or dress. For example, if the accused were to give a false impression by suggesting he was a priest by wearing a clerical collar.

The accused is treated as being responsible for an assertion which gives a false or misleading impression where:

(i) He makes the assertion himself, either in his evidence or in his representative's presentation of his case;

(ii) He made the assertion when being questioned under caution or on being charged with the offence;

(iii) The assertion is made by a defence witness when responding to a question by the accused that was designed (or likely to) elicit it; and

(iv) It was made out of court by anyone and the accused adduces evidence of it.

If the accused withdraws or disassociates himself from the false impression, the prosecution will not be permitted to call evidence of his bad character under this provision.

In correcting the impression, the prosecution may only introduce such probative evidence of the accused's misconduct as is necessary to correct the false impression. Exactly what evidence is admissible will depend on the facts of the case.

(g) The accused has attacked another person's character

Only the prosecution may adduce evidence of the accused's bad character under this provision. Evidence which attacks a person's character is that which shows that the person has committed an offence or has behaved in a reprehensible way. Thus, an accused would be attacking a prosecution witness if he claimed that they were lying in their version of events or he adduced evidence of their previous misconduct to undermine their credibility. The provision does not apply where it is merely suggested that a witness is mistaken.

An accused attacks another person's character if:

(i) He adduces evidence attacking their character;

(ii) He (or his legal representative appointed under YJCEA 1999, s.38) cross-examines in such a way as is designed (or likely) to elicit such evidence;

(iii) He makes an imputation (an allegation of this nature) when questioned under caution or on being charged with the offence or officially informed that he might be prosecuted for it and this is heard in evidence.

Exclusionary Duty Where this provision applies, the accused can apply to have evidence of his bad character excluded if it would have such an adverse effect on the fairness of the trial that it ought to be excluded (s.101(3)) (see above).

Stopping the case where evidence contaminated

Where evidence of the accused's bad character is admitted under any of the provisions (c) to (g) above, the court must either direct an acquittal or discharge the jury and order a retrial if, at any time following the close of the prosecution case, it is satisfied that the evidence is contaminated and the contamination is such that, in view of the importance of the evidence to the prosecution's case, the conviction would be unsafe (s.107).

A person's evidence is contaminated where it is false or misleading or is different from what it would otherwise have been in consequence of: (a) an agreement or understanding between that person and one or more others; or (b) the person being aware of something alleged by another person(s) who has testified in the proceedings.

EVIDENCE OF THE BAD CHARACTER OF SOMEONE OTHER THAN THE ACCUSED

Section 100 sets out the circumstances in which evidence can be given of the previous misconduct of a person other than the accused in the proceedings. This might be a witness or a victim but could be anyone. Such evidence is only admissible if:

(a) It is important explanatory evidence; or
(b) It is of substantial probative value to a matter in issue and that issue is one of substantial importance in the case; or
(c) The prosecution and defence agree that the evidence should be admitted.

Important explanatory evidence

See above.

Evidence of substantial probative value to a matter in issue which is one of substantial importance in the case

Evidence is of probative value to a matter in issue where it helps to prove that issue. Evidence of the bad character of a witness may be probative, for example, where the credibility of the witness is questioned because this is likely to affect the court's assessment of the issue on which the witness testifies or where it is used to support the accused's assertion that someone else committed the offence.

Only evidence which is of substantial probative value is admissible and only then if the matter to which it relates is of substantial importance in the case.

In assessing this probative value, s.100(3) directs the court to take into account any relevant factors and, specifically:

(i) The nature and number of the events to which it relates and when those events occurred;

(ii) Where the evidence is of misconduct that is tendered as probative evidence because of its similarity with other evidence in the case (for example, to suggest that the victim behaved in a particular way), the nature and extent of the similarities and dissimilarities;

(iii) Where the evidence is of misconduct and it is adduced to suggest that a person (whose identity is disputed) was responsible for the offence for which the accused is being tried, the extent to which the evidence shows or tends to show that the same person was responsible each time.

The prosecution and defence agree that the evidence should be admitted

This is self-explanatory.

[*Note:* leave is required to adduce evidence in situations (a) and (b) above but not where the prosecution and defence agree that the evidence should be admitted.]

Assessment of relevance or probative value

When the court is required to assess the relevance or probative value of evidence, it does so on the assumption that the evidence is true unless, on the material before it, no court or jury could reasonably find it to be true (s.109). If the evidence is admitted, the judge must direct the jury that they may only rely on the evidence for a purpose adverse to the accused if satisfied that it is true (*R. v H* (1995)).

Court's duty to give reasons for its rulings

Where the court makes a ruling under s.107 or that an item of evidence is evidence of a person's bad character and that such evidence is admissible under s.100 or 101, it must give its reasons for the ruling in open court (s.110).

Evidence of character in civil proceedings (similar fact evidence)

Essentially, evidence of bad character is admissible as "similar fact evidence" in civil proceedings if it is relevant to an issue in the proceedings (*Mood Music v De Wolfe* (1976)). Thus, for example, where the claimant asserts that the defendant has infringed his copyright in a musical work, evidence of other such infringements on the defendant's behalf may be admissible because it is relevant in determining whether the similarities between the claimant's musical work and the defendant's musical work were a coincidence (*Mood Music v De Wolfe*). Where such evidence is relevant, however, the court still possesses discretion to exclude it (under Rule 32.1 of the Civil Procedure Rules 1998), for example if it is of limited probative value and would add to the complexity or expense of the proceedings (*O'Brien v Chief Constable of the South Wales Police* (2003)).

14. SAMPLE QUESTIONS AND MODEL ANSWERS

[*Note:* this chapter is written as though the evidence provisions of the Criminal Justice Act 2003 are already in force. The relevant provisions are due to be brought into force in 2005.]

QUESTION 1

Frank and Michael are jointly charged with Arson and both intend to plead not guilty. The prosecution allege that the two co-accused set fire to a barn belonging to Diana. Frank's defence is alibi; Frank asserting that at the time when the fire started he was at home with his girlfriend, Freda. Michael admits that he and Frank were in the barn with Diana when the fire started but asserts that, whilst Diana and Frank started the fire as part of an insurance fraud, he (Michael) was not involved. Diana asserts that whilst she tried to stop them doing so, Frank and Michael set fire to her barn against her wishes. Frank does not intend to testify in his defence. Michael does intend to testify in his defence and intends to call Reverend Adams who will testify that Michael is a lay preacher at his church who regularly takes part in sponsored activities to raise funds for the new church roof. Frank has a previous conviction for arson and two for offences of dishonesty. Michael has no previous convictions. Diana has a previous conviction for handling stolen goods.

(a) Consider whether Frank can be compelled to testify and, if not, what the potential consequences of his failure to testify might be.
(b) Consider the admissibility of the evidence of Michael's good character.
(c) Consider the admissibility of the previous convictions of Frank and Diana.

Answer

(a) Frank, being charged with an offence in the proceedings, is a competent but not compellable defence witness (Criminal Evidence Act 1898, s.1). In other words, Frank can choose to testify in his defence but cannot be required to do so. Frank, being charged with an offence in the proceedings, is not a competent witness for the prosecution (Youth Justice and Criminal Evidence Act 1999, s.53). Thus, Frank cannot be called to give evidence for the prosecution.

If Frank decides not to testify in his defence, this gives rise to the possibility that the jury may be entitled to draw an inference in respect of his failure under s.35 of the Criminal Justice and Public Order Act 1994. Essentially the jury will be entitled to draw such an inference provided that Frank's physical or mental condition does not make it undesirable for him to testify. In order for an inference to be drawn under s.35, the evidence before the jury must raise a prima facie case against Frank. Moreover, Frank cannot be convicted solely or mainly upon the basis of a s.35 inference and the jury should not draw such an inference unless they are sure that he failed to testify either because he had no answer to the charges against him or had none that would withstand cross-examination. The burden of proof remains on the prosecution throughout the trial and s.35 does not remove the accused's right of silence. The judge's directions to the jury must make them aware of the abovementioned matters (*R. v Cowan*) and the nature of his directions will be crucial as, in the context of a misdirection, there may be the potential for a violation of the right to a fair trial guaranteed by Art.6 of the European Convention on Human Rights (*Condron v UK*). In exceptional circumstances, the judge might be prepared to exercise his exclusionary discretion (*i.e.* under s.78 of the Police and Criminal Evidence Act 1984) to prevent the drawing of a s.35 inference (*R. v Cowan*).

(b) In relation to the issue of Michael's good character, the extent to which the accused may adduce evidence of his own good character is governed by the common law authority of *R. v Rowton*. In this case the court held that only evidence of the accused's general reputation in the community would be permitted, evidence of specific examples of good deeds or the witness's opinion of the accused would not. Applying the rule in *Rowton*, the Reverend Adams would be allowed to state that Michael is a lay preacher as this would be generally known. Strictly, applying *Rowton*, the Reverend Adams should not be permitted to state that Michael regularly raises funds for the new church roof as this is a specific example of Michael's good character. Since *Rowton* was decided, however, a slightly more flexible approach has been adopted by the courts, as illustrated in *R. v Redgrave*, so it is possible that the trial judge might permit Reverend Adams to comment upon Michael's fund-raising activities, but this is uncertain.

Should the Reverend Adams be permitted to give evidence of Michael's good character, such evidence will be relevant both to Michael's guilt, *i.e.* to show that, as a person of good character, he is unlikely to have committed the offence with which he is charged and to his credit, *i.e.* to show that he is more likely to tell the truth under oath (*R. v Vye*). Michael will be entitled to a direction from the judge to the jury to this effect even though he is jointly charged with Frank who is of bad character (*R. v Vye*).

(c) The admissibility of evidence of bad character in criminal proceedings is governed by provisions of the Criminal Justice

Act 2003. Essentially, for the purposes of these provisions, "evidence of bad character" is evidence of, or of a disposition towards, misconduct (s.98) and misconduct means the commission of an offence or other reprehensible behaviour (s.112). Evidence of bad character does not include evidence which has to do with the alleged facts of the offence with which the accused is charged or evidence of misconduct in connection with the investigation or prosecution of that offence (s.98). Thus, the previous convictions of Frank and Diana amount to evidence of bad character for the purposes of the 2003 Act's character provisions but the alleged facts of the offence with which Frank and Michael are charged do not amount to evidence of bad character for this purpose.

Frank's convictions will only be admissible if one or more of paragraphs (a) to (g) of s.101(1) of the 2003 Act are applicable. It is unlikely that paragraphs (a) or (b) will apply as, respectively, there seems to be no reason why Frank would agree to the admission of evidence of his convictions or would want to adduce such evidence himself.

[*Note:* if it becomes clear to the defence that the prosecution will be entitled to adduce evidence of Frank's convictions under one or more of the other paragraphs of s.101(1) but they have not already been adduced in evidence by the time when Frank testifies, Frank may decide that it would be beneficial for his counsel to adduce evidence of his convictions more sympathetically from him under s.101(1)(b).]

Paragraph (c) does not appear to be relevant as his convictions do not appear to be relevant for the purpose of enabling the jury to understand other facts in the case.

Under paragraph (d), the the question for the judge will be whether the convictions are relevant to an important matter in issue between Frank and the prosecution. The important matter may include evidence of the accused's propensity to commit offences of the type with which he is charged (unless the evidence makes his guilt no more likely) and may include evidence of his propensity to be untruthful (unless it is not suggested that his case is untruthful (s.103)). Whilst the accused's propensity to commit offences may be established in a variety of ways, two ways or proving it are either by proving that he has been convicted of an offence of the same description as that with which he is charged (*e.g.* a rape conviction in the context of a rape trial) or by proving that he has been convicted of an offence of the same category as that with which he is charged (s.103).

[*Note:* at the time of writing the categories had not yet been prescribed by the Secretary of State.]

It appears that Frank's arson conviction will fall within s.101(1)(d). If the facts of the offence with which Frank is charged and those of the offence of which he is convicted are similar, the arson conviction may have substantial probative value in relation to an issue in the proceedings, such as negating the defence of innocent association. Even if this is not so, it appears that the arson conviction will still be relevant to the issue of his propensity to commit an offence of the same description as that which he is charged and that it may be relied upon to prove the existence of that propensity. It should be noted, however, that if the defence make an application under s.101(3), the judge should exclude the rape conviction if its admission would have such an adverse effect on the fairness of the trial that it ought to be excluded. In reaching his decision, the matters that the judge should take into account include the time that has elapsed between the previous events and the current charge.

In relation to Frank's dishonesty convictions, they are clearly not relevant under s.101(1)(d) to show that he has a propensity to commit arson, but, presumably, may be relevant as evidence of his propensity to be untruthful. Again, if the defence make an application under s.101(3), the judge should exclude the dishonesty convictions if their admission would have such an adverse effect on the fairness of the trial that they ought to be excluded.

Frank claims that he was not at the scene of the crime; Michael claims that he and Frank were present but asserts that whilst Diana and Frank were involved in its commission, he (Michael) was not. Paragraph 101(1)(e) thus appears to be applicable in the context of Frank's dishonesty convictions because it seems that Frank's defence undermines Michael's defence in that if Frank's defence is true, at least part of Michael's version of the facts must be a lie. Thus, it is submitted that Frank's dishonesty convictions, in providing evidence of his propensity to be untruthful, do possess substantial probative value in relation to an important matter in issue between Frank and Michael. Arguably, the arson conviction does not appear to have any relevance to an important matter in issue between Frank and Michael as whilst it potentially makes Frank's involvement in the offence more likely it does not make it less likely that Michael was involved. It should be noted that whilst the court always possesses discretion (under s.78 of the Police and Evidence Act 1984) to exclude evidence tendered by the prosecution, including evidence of the accused's bad character, the admission of which would adversely effect the fairness of the proceedings such that it should be excluded, the s.78 discretion is inapplicable to evidence tendered under s.101(1)(e), as this is defence evidence.

So far as we are aware, Frank has not given a false impression about himself and therefore s.101(1)(f) does not appear to be relevant. Finally, Frank has not made an attack on another person's character, so s.101(1)(g) does not appear to apply.

Finally, in relation to Diana's handling conviction, the conviction will only be admissible, under s.100, if it is important explanatory evidence, it has of substantial probative value in relation to a matter in issue which is of substantial importance in the case or by agreement between the parties. Moreover, other than where such evidence is admitted by agreement, the leave of the court will be required if the handling conviction is to be admitted. Here, the evidence does not appear to be important explanatory evidence (*i.e.* it does not appear to assist the court to properly understand other evidence) but, being a dishonesty conviction, it may arguably have substantial probative value in relation to the credibility of Diana, which does appear to be a matter of substantial importance.

QUESTION 2

Sylvia has been charged with criminal damage to her boyfriend's car. The prosecution allege that, upon finding out that Dave, her boyfriend, was also seeing his secretary behind her back, Sylvia went to Dave's office car park and poured paint stripper all over his brand new Mercedes, causing extensive damage. Sylvia denies damaging the car. The prosecution wish to rely upon the following items of evidence:

(1) Sylvia's admission when questioned by the police that she had damaged the car;
(2) The evidence of Bill, an elderly car park attendant, who saw a woman whom he described as being petite, in her late thirties and with long blonde hair near the car (which

was about 50 metres away) shortly before it was damaged. However, he was called away and did not see the actual damage occur. Bill later identified Sylvia at an identification parade as the woman he had seen near the car.

Sylvia is aged 23, has medium length mousy hair and is five feet nine inches tall. She says that she only admitted damaging the car because she is a diabetic and had been held at the police station for 24 hours without access to her insulin. She felt unwell and was anxious to get home for an injection of insulin but did not inform the police about her diabetes as she has always been acutely embarrassed about her illness and refuses to tell anyone about it. She had asked to see a solicitor but he was delayed and the police continued to question her in his absence. She confessed to the offence before her solicitor arrived. Advise the prosecution as to:

(i) the admissibility of Sylvia's admission; and
(ii) any evidential problems associated with the use of Bill's evidence.

Answer

Sylvia's admission   Sylvia's admission at the police station amounts to a confession, being adverse to her interests (PACE 1984, s.82(1)). As Sylvia admits making the confession but denies committing the offence, the issue of the admissibility of the confession will be heard on a *voir dire*. The confession will not be admissible unless the prosecution can prove beyond a reasonable doubt that the confession was not obtained as a result of oppression or in consequence of anything said or done which, in the circumstances existing at the time, was likely to render unreliable any confession which Sylvia might make in consequence thereof (s.76(2)(a) & (b) of PACE 1984). Thus, it is the manner in which the prosecution obtained the confession which is relevant, not whether the confession may be true (*R. v Crampton*).

As the prosecution must first prove that the confession was not obtained by oppression, it is necessary to define this term. Oppression has a partial definition in s.76(8) as including ". . . torture, inhuman or degrading treatment, and the use or threat of violence (whether or not amounting to torture)." Clearly, Sylvia was not subjected to such treatment at the police station.

However, as the statutory definition is not an all-encompassing definition, the courts have provided their own definition. In *R. v Fulling*, the court gave the word its Oxford English Dictionary meaning which is, the "Exercise of authority in a burdensome, harsh or wrongful manner; unjust or cruel treatment of subjects, inferiors, etc.; the imposition of unreasonable or unjust burdens." Lord Lane C.J. took the view that improper conduct on the part of the interviewer was an essential ingredient of oppression as defined above. Sylvia has not had access to her insulin and was questioned in the absence of her solicitor. The failure to provide insulin would not constitute oppression as the police officers were not aware she was a diabetic and so there was no impropriety on their part in this regard. As for the questioning in the absence of her solicitor, the court stated, *obiter*, in *R. v Alladice*, that refusal to allow access to a solicitor, if accompanied by bad faith, might constitute oppression. Although a solicitor was in fact called in this case, Sylvia was questioned before he arrived which, unless properly authorised (of which there is no suggestion in the question), is contrary to s.58 of PACE. The court may treat this the same as if the police had refused to let Sylvia call a solicitor and, if the police acted in bad faith, this may amount to oppression. If it does, the confession will be excluded unless the prosecution can prove beyond a reasonable doubt that the confession was not obtained by the oppression, *i.e.* there was no casual link between the two.

Should the court determine that there was no oppression, or that if there was oppression that there was no casual link between the oppression and the confession, the prosecution must then prove that the confession was not obtained in consequence of anything said or done which (in the circumstances existing at the time) was likely to render any confession so obtained unreliable (s.76(2)(b)). There is no statutory definition of unreliability but it is clear that impropriety is not required (*Fulling*). In approaching s.76(2)(b), the court must consider three issues:

  (i) whether anything relevant was said or done;
  (ii) the circumstances existing at the time; and
  (iii) whether in those circumstances, the thing said or done was likely to render any confession unreliable.

On the facts, the something said or done could be the questioning in the absence of a solicitor (*Alladice*). The failure to provide insulin could not constitute something said or done as the interviewing officers were unaware of Sylvia's diabetes (*R. v Goldenberg*). Her diabetes could, however, constitute a circumstance, despite the officers' ignorance of Sylvia's condition (*R. v Everett*), as could her lack of legal advice. Should the court determine that something was said or done, the prosecution must prove beyond a reasonable doubt either that the accused did not confess in consequence of it or that it was not likely to render any confession unreliable. If they fail to do so, the confession will be excluded.

If the confession is not excluded under s.76, it may still be excluded by the judge in the exercise of his discretion, either at common law or under s.78 of PACE. Section 82(3) preserves the discretion which existed at common law but since the enactment of PACE, the courts have tended to rely on their exclusionary discretion under s.78. Section 78 permits the judge to exclude a confession if he considers that, having regard to all the circumstances, including the circumstances in which it was made, it would have such an adverse effect on the fairness of the proceedings that the judge ought not to admit it. In deciding whether to exercise his discretion, the judge may take into account the fact that there was a breach of PACE or the Codes of Practice. The police in this question appear to have breached s.58 of PACE. In *R. v Walsh*, the court stated that if there was a significant or substantial breach of PACE or the Codes of Practice then prima facie the necessary standard of fairness has not been met but the breach must have such an adverse effect on the proceedings before the confession will be excluded. Breach of s.58 is likely to be treated as a significant and substantial breach, the right to access to a solicitor being described in *R. v Samuel* as "fundamental". If the judge is satisfied that Sylvia would probably not have confessed had questioning been delayed until her solicitor arrived, he is likely to exercise his discretion to exclude (*Samuel*). If the judge is not satisfied of this, he may still exclude if the police officers' decision to continue questioning amounted to a deliberate decision not to comply with the requirements of PACE (*Alladice*).

Bill's identification of Sylvia Bill has positively identified Sylvia at an ID parade, an ID which Sylvia disputes. Thus, the *Turnbull* ID guidelines will apply. The judge must warn the jury of the special need for caution when deciding whether to place reliance upon the evidence of an identification witness and explain to them that an ID witness may, though very convincing, still be mistaken. The judge should direct the jury to consider the circumstances in which the witness observed the accused, pointing out any weaknesses and discrepancies between the description given by the witness and the actual appearance of the accused. On the facts of this case, the judge should point out to the jury the discrepancies in terms of Sylvia's age, height and length and colour of hair and also direct them to consider whether Bill's eyesight may not be particularly good given his age and whether, at a distance of 50m, he could have clearly seen the person standing next to the car. The ID evidence in this case appears poor and, if there was no other evidence to support the identification, the judge would be obliged, under the guidelines, to withdraw the case from the jury and direct an acquittal. The ID is supported by Sylvia's confession, if it is admissible. If the confession is excluded, however, the judge may be required to direct an acquittal, in the absence of other supporting evidence.

QUESTION 3

Henry has been charged with the murder of Mandy and is pleading not guilty. The prosecution allege that Henry shot Mandy, his estranged wife, as she walked home from her night class. Henry denies that he saw Mandy on the evening when she was killed. The prosecution wish to call Jane, who also attended the night class, who will testify that as she left the night class she saw a man walk up to Mandy and Mandy said "Hello Henry, what do you want?". The prosecution also wish to call Tom who will testify that, he found Mandy after she had been shot and, before she lapsed into unconsciousness, she said to Tom, "It was my husband Henry who shot me". Finally, the prosecution wish to adduce in evidence the notebook of PC Plodd, a police officer. PC Plodd attended Mandy in hospital, several days after the shooting, during a brief period when she was conscious and wrote down in his notebook Mandy's statement in which she named Henry as her assailant. Mandy died shortly after making this statement and P.C. Plodd was killed later on the same day whilst trying to prevent a bank robbery.

Advise the prosecution as to the admissibility of the evidence of Jane, Tom and the notebook of PC Plodd.

Answer

The evidence of Jane Essentially, a hearsay statement is a statement not made in oral evidence in the proceedings which is relied upon as evidence of a matter stated (see Criminal Justice Act 2003, s.114). Subject to the exceptions recognized by s.114 of the Criminal Justice Act 2003 (which are considered below), hearsay evidence is not admissible in criminal proceedings. Jane's evidence is not a hearsay statement, however, because it is not relied upon as evidence of a matter stated. This is so because, under s.115(3), the hearsay provisions of the 2003 Act do not apply to a matter stated unless at least one of the purposes of the maker of the statement is either to cause a person to believe the matter stated or to cause a person to act or a machine to operate upon the basis that the matter is as stated. Here, it does not appear that when Mandy said "Hello Henry" that she did so with the purpose of making anyone believe that the man to whom she was talking was called Henry (or making a person act or a machine operate upon that basis). Consequently, if the prosecution wish to rely upon Mandy's statement as evidence identifying the man she met as Henry, it is submitted that the statement is not hearsay evidence and is admissible for this purpose.

The Evidence of Tom Mandy's statement to Tom was not made whilst she was giving oral evidence in the proceedings and, presumably, will be relied upon by the prosecution as evidence of the matters stated (*i.e.* to prove that it was Henry who murdered her). Thus, it appears that the statement is a hearsay statement and will only be admissible under s.114 of the Criminal Justice Act 2003 if the parties agree to its admission, if it is admissible under a statutory exception to the hearsay rule, if it is admissible under a preserved common law exception to the hearsay rule or if the court admits it in the exercise of its inclusionary discretion under s.114(1)(d). The statement might be admissible under a common law exception to the hearsay rule, preserved by s.118 of the 2003 Act, as forming part of the *res gestae*. Specifically, it might be admissible upon the basis that Mandy was so emotionally overpowered by the stabbing at the time when she made the statement that the possibility of concoction or distortion can be disregarded. When considering the admissibility of the evidence, the trial judge should pay particular attention to any factors which might increase the risk of concoction (such as whether the maker had a grudge against the accused) and to any special factors which might give rise to the possibility of error (*e.g.* whether the maker was intoxicated at the time when she made the statement) (*R. v Andrews*). Mandy's statement was made shortly after the stabbing. Tom may repeat it in court provided that the judge (taking into account any factors which may give rise to an increased risk of fabrication and of any special factors giving rise to a risk of error) is satisfied that Mandy's mind was dominated by the shooting at the time when she made it.

The statement may also be admissible under s.116 of the Criminal Justice Act 2003. Essentially, this will be the case if Mandy could have given oral evidence of the matter stated, she is identified to the court's satisfaction and one of the s.116 reasons for not calling Mandy is satisfied. Here, there appears to be no reason why Mandy's oral evidence of the matters stated would not have been admissible, it appears that she can be identified to the court's satisfaction and one of the s.116 reasons for not calling her is satisfied, *i.e.* she is dead. Thus, the statement appears to be admissible under s.116.

It should be noted that the trial judge possesses discretion to exclude evidence tendered by the prosecution in the exercise of his discretion under s.78 of the Police and Criminal Evidence Act 1984 if its admission would adversely effect the fairness of the trial such that it should be excluded. If admitting the hearsay evidence would render the accused's trial unfair for the purposes of Art.6 of the European Convention on Human Rights (which gives the accused the right to examine (or have examined) the witnesses for the prosecution), it is submitted that the judge should, in compliance with his duty under s.3 of the Human Rights Act 1998, exclude the hearsay evidence under s.78. In determining whether admitting the hearsay statement for the prosecution is likely to give rise to a violation of Art.6, it appears that the matters the court will need to consider will include whether the hearsay evidence forms the sole or main evidence of the accused's guilt, whether the defence have had the opportunity to adduce other evidence contradicting the hearsay evidence and whether the defence have had an opportunity to discredit the maker of the hearsay statement (*Triverdi v UK*).

PC Plodd's notebook

Mandy's statement to PC Plodd was not made whilst she was giving oral evidence in the proceedings and, presumably, will be relied upon by the prosecution as evidence of the matters stated (*i.e.* to prove that it was Henry who murdered her). Thus, it appears that the statement is a hearsay statement and will only be admissible, under s.114 of the Criminal Justice Act 2003 if the parties agree to its admission, if it is admissible under a statutory exception to the hearsay rule, if it is admissible under a preserved common law exception to the hearsay rule or if the court admits it in the exercise of its inclusionary discretion under s.114(1)(d).

The preserved common law *res gestae* hearsay exception, considered above, does not appear to apply to the hearsay statement contained in the notebook because, after several days, it appears to be unlikely that Mandy would still have been so emotionally overpowered by the stabbing that the possibility of concoction or distortion can be disregarded. The Criminal Justice Act 2003 s.116 hearsay exception, also considered above, appears to apply because there appears to be no reason why Mandy's oral evidence of the matters stated would not have been admissible, it appears that she can be identified to the court's satisfaction and one of the s.116 reasons for not calling her is satisfied, *i.e.* she is dead. Finally, the hearsay exception created by s.117 of the 2003 Act also appears to apply because the statement is contained in a document, oral evidence would be admissible to prove the matters stated, the supplier of information (Mandy) presumably had personal knowledge of the matters stated and the person who created the document (PC Plodd) did so as the holder of the office of constable. Because the statement was presumably prepared for the purposes of a criminal investigation it appears that one of the statutory reasons for not calling Mandy must be satisfied, but since she is dead this is not a problem. It should be noted, however, that, under s.117(6),(7), the court possesses discretion to determine that the hearsay statement will not be admissible under s.117 if satisfied that its reliability is doubtful. More generally, as was indicated above, when determining whether to exclude the statement either under the s.117(6)(7) exclusionary discretion or in the exercise of the exclusionary discretion conferred by s.78 of the Police and Criminal Evidence Act 1984 (which will also be applicable if the evidence is admissible at common law or under s.116 of the 2003 Act), it is submitted that the court should consider whether admitting the relevant evidence for the prosecution would give rise to a violation of Art.6 of the European Convention on Human Rights.

Finally, it should be noted that, under s.133 of the 2003 Act, a statement contained in a document may be proved either by producing the original or by producing a copy, authenticated in a manner approved by the court. Here, the original notebook is available and, consequently, the statement may be proved by producing it.

QUESTION 4

Fred is charged with two counts of rape. Specifically, he is charged with raping his two daughters, Barbara, aged 17, and Julie, aged 13. The girls allege that, during the year before their father left home to live with his girlfriend, Sonya, he had, on different occasions, raped both of them. Both daughters claim that neither they nor their mother, Audrey, dared to inform the police of their father's conduct because he had threatened to kill them all if they did so. When Fred was taken to the police station for questioning, he was given the opportunity to consult a solicitor but chose not to. He was questioned under caution but refused to say anything. At trial, Fred intends to deny the charges against him and assert that he had virtually lived with Sonya in the year before he left the marital home and had been with her at her house on all the occasions when it is alleged that he raped his daughters.

The counts relating to Barbara and Julie are being jointly tried in Oxgate Crown Court. Consider whether:

(a) Julie is likely to be a competent prosecution witness;
(b) Audrey can be compelled to testify for the prosecution;
(c) The jury are likely to be permitted to consider the evidence relating to the alleged rape of Barbara upon the trial of the count relating to Julie and whether they are likely to be permitted to consider the evidence relating to the alleged rape of Julie upon the trial of the count relating to Barbara;
(d) There are any evidential implications of Fred's silence when questioned by the police;
(e) The trial judge is required to warn the jury of the danger of relying upon the evidence of any or all of Audrey, Barbara and Julie;

  (f) Fred will be entitled to personally cross-examine Barbara
       and Julie;
  (g) Evidence of Barbara's sexual experience with other men
       will be admissible in Fred's defence.

Answer

(a) A witness is competent if the court may receive the witness's
testimony. A witness is compellable if the witness may be
required to testify. In criminal proceedings, under s.53 of the
Youth Justice and Criminal Evidence Act 1999, all persons are
competent witnesses. Julie is under 14 years of age and, consequently, under s.55 of the Youth Justice and Criminal Evidence
Act 1999, she may not give sworn evidence. Even though Julie
cannot give sworn evidence, she may give unsworn evidence
under s.56 of the 1999 Act if she is a competent witness.

Under s.53 of the 1999 Act, Julie will not be a competent
witness if it appears to the court that she cannot understand
questions put to her and give answers to those questions which
can be understood. If the issue of Julie's competence is raised,
either by the court or by one of the parties, s.54 of the 1999 Act
provides that the party who called her (*i.e.* the prosecution)
bears the burden of proving on the balance of probabilities that
she is competent. Section 54 also provides that proceedings to
determine Julie's competence will take place in the absence of
the jury, that expert evidence may be received for the purpose
of determining her competence and that any questioning of Julie
for this purpose will be conducted by the judge. Finally, s.54
provides that where the court gives or intends to give a special
measures direction in relation to a witness, the court must take
this into account when determining the witness's competence.

In Julie's case, a special measure direction will be required
under the 1999 Act because Julie will be a child witness who is
in need of special protection. Thus, her evidence in chief will be
video recorded and cross-examination and re-examination will
also be video recorded unless Julie objects, in which case they
will be by TV live link. Video recorded evidence will not be
admitted, however, if this is not in the interests of justice.

In practice, at the age of 13, Julie is likely to be a competent
witness, and thus will also be compellable, to give unsworn
evidence by video recording.

(b) In general, the spouse of the accused is a competent prosecution witness but cannot be compelled to testify (Youth Justice

and Criminal Evidence Act 1999, s.53; Police and Criminal Evidence Act 1984, s.80).

The spouse is not a competent prosecution witness if the spouse is charged with an offence in the proceedings (s.53). The spouse is a compellable prosecution witness if the offence with which the accused is charged falls within s.80(3) of the 1984 Act. The offences with which Fred is charged do fall within s.80(3) (they are sexual offences allegedly committed in respect of persons who were under 16 years of age at the material time).

Thus, Audrey appears to be a competent and compellable prosecution witness.

(c) The question is whether the evidence of each daughter is likely to be admissible as evidence of bad character in relation to the trial of the count relating to the other. The admissibility of evidence of bad character in criminal proceedings is governed by provisions of the Criminal Justice Act 2003. Essentially, for the purposes of these provisions, "evidence of bad character" is evidence of, or of a disposition towards, misconduct (s.98) and misconduct means the commission of an offence or other reprehensible behaviour (s.112). Evidence of bad character does not include evidence which has to do with the alleged facts of the offence with which the accused is charged or evidence of misconduct in connection with the investigation or prosecution of that offence (s.98). The effect of s.112(2) is, however, that where the accused is charged with several offences, evidence of the facts of one offence will amount to evidence of bad character when the court is considering whether it is admissible in relation to one or more of the other offences with which the accused is charged. Thus, when the court is considering whether Fred raped Barbara, the alleged facts of the alleged rape of Barbara will not amount to evidence of Fred's bad character for the purposes of the character provisions of the 2003 Act but when the court is considering whether Fred raped Julie, the alleged facts of the alleged rape of Barbara will amount to evidence of Fred's bad character for the purposes of the character provisions of the 2003 Act. Thus, evidence of the alleged facts of the alleged rape of Barbara will only be admissible to prove that Fred raped Julie if one or more of paragraphs (a) to (g) of s.101(1) of the 2003 Act is applicable. Similarly, evidence of the alleged facts of the alleged rape of Julie will only be admissible to prove that Fred raped Barbara if one or more of paragraphs (a) to (g) of s.101(1) of the 2003 Act is applicable.

The provision of s.101(1) which appears to be potentially applicable upon these facts appears to be s.101(1)(d). Under s.101(1)(d), question for the judge will be whether the evidence relating to one count (*e.g.* to the offence allegedly committed in respect of Barbara) is relevant to an important matter in issue between Fred and the prosecution in relation to the other account (*e.g.* in relation to the offence allegedly committed in respect of Julie). The important matter may include evidence of the accused's propensity to commit offences of the type with which he is charged (unless the evidence makes his guilt no more likely) and may include evidence of his propensity to be untruthful (unless it is not suggested that his case is untruthful) (s.103)). Whilst the accused's propensity to commit offences may be established in a variety of ways, two ways or proving it are either by proving that he has been convicted of an offence of the same description as that with which he is charged (*e.g.* a rape conviction in the context of a rape trial) or by proving that he has been convicted of an offence of the same category as that with which he is charged (s.103).

[*Note:* at the time of writing the categories had not yet been prescribed by the Secretary of State.]

If Fred suggests that Barbara and Julie have colluded to fabricate their evidence against him, the effect of s.109 of the 2003 Act is that (unless it appears upon the basis of material before the judge, that no court or jury could reasonably find their evidence to be true), the judge should determine the relevance of the evidence of bad character upon the basis of the assumption that it is true. The evidence being admitted, it will then normally be for the jury to determine whether it is true (*R. v H*).

(d) When he was taken to the police station, Fred was given the opportunity to consult a solicitor but chose not to. He was questioned under caution but failed to mention the fact that he was with his girlfriend, Sonya, when the alleged rapes occurred. This fact was one which he could reasonably have been expected to mention and which he wishes to rely upon at trial. Thus, all the requirements of s.34 of the Criminal Justice and Public Order Act 1994 are satisfied. This will permit the court in determining guilt (subject to the trial judge's exclusionary discretion, (s.38(6)), to draw such inferences as appear proper from the failure to mention this fact. The inference which the court may draw is either that Fred has made up the story about being with Sonya when the alleged rapes occurred since he was questioned by the police or, that he had already begun to fabricate this alibi when he was interviewed but was unwilling to mention it as he had not had the chance to think it through sufficiently to expose it to detailed questioning (*R. v Randall*).

When directing the jury on s.34, the judge should, amongst other matters, make clear to them that

(a) Fred cannot be convicted solely or mainly upon an inference drawn under s.34 (*Murray v UK*); and

(b) They may not draw an inference unless they are satisfied both that the requirements of s.34 have been met and that Fred's silence can only sensibly be attributed to his having no answer to the charges against him or none which would withstand questioning and investigation (*R. v Betts*).

If the trial judge fails to direct the jury on all these matters, this may result in a violation of Fred's right to a fair trial under Art.6 of the Convention (*Condron v UK*).

(e) A trial judge is no longer required to give the jury a corroboration warning in respect of the evidence of children (Criminal Justice Act 1988, s.34(2)), accomplices or sexual offence complainants (Criminal Justice and Public Order Act 1994, s.32(1)). The role of the trial judge following this statutory reform was considered by the Court of Appeal in *R. v Makanjuola*.

Essentially, it appears that whilst the judge may give a warning he is not required to do so merely because Barbara and Julie are sexual offence complainants or because Julie is a child. Rather, a warning should only be given if there is an evidential basis for suggesting that a witness is unreliable.

In this case, the fact that Jack left Audrey for another woman may provide an evidential basis for the suggestion that Audrey and her two daughters have a grudge against Fred. Consequently, the judge may feel that it is necessary to warn the jury to be cautious when relying on the evidence of Barbara or on that of either daughter. If he is particularly concerned that the evidence may be unreliable, the judge may go further and advise the jury to look for evidence supporting the potentially unreliable evidence before relying on it. Any such supporting evidence must be independent of the witness whose evidence requires support (*R. v Islam*).

(f) Under s.36 of the Youth Justice and Criminal Evidence Act 1999, an accused charged with a sexual offence is not permitted to personally cross-examine the complainant. Fred will, however, be permitted to instruct counsel to cross-examine Julie on his behalf and, if he fails or refuses to do so, the court may, in the interests of justice, appoint a qualified legal representative (under s.38) to cross-examine Barbara and Julie.

(g) Under s.41 of the Youth Justice and Criminal Evidence Act 1999, evidence of Barbara's sexual behaviour (which does not include the facts of the alleged rape itself) will not be admissible without the leave of the court, which can only be given either if the evidence is relevant to an issue other than consent, or in certain specified circumstances if the evidence is relevant to consent. Moreover, leave can only be given if failing to give it might render a conclusion of the jury unsafe. Here, so far as we can tell, evidence of Barbara's sexual experience with other men does not appear to be relevant to any issue in the proceedings, whether or not one of consent, and does not appear to relate to any evidence adduced by the prosecution in relation to her sexual behaviour. In particular, it should be noted that when determining whether evidence of Barbara's sexual behaviour is relevant to an issue in the proceedings for the purposes of s.41, evidence of her sexual behaviour will not relate to such an issue if the sole or main purpose for adducing it is merely to discredit Barbara. Thus, so far as we can tell, it appears that evidence of Barbara's sexual experience with other men will not be admissible.

QUESTION 5

Jack, a travelling salesman, is bringing a claim for negligence against Amanda in respect of an accident in which his car was damaged when he swerved and left the road in order to avoid a car driven by Amanda which was heading towards him on the wrong side of the road. Immediately after Jack swerved, Amanda collided with a car driven by Tom, both her car and the car driven by Tom being damaged in the collision. The claim has been allocated to the fast track.

Following the accident, Amanda was convicted of dangerous driving by Oxgate Crown Court. Tom then successfully brought a claim for negligence against her, recovering damages in respect of the damage to his car.

Amanda claims that Jack's accident was not her fault because, immediately prior to it, the steering of her car had failed and this had caused her car to veer onto the other carriageway. Further, Amanda has obtained possession of a letter concerning the accident, written by Jack to his solicitor, Eric, in which Jack stated,

> "I had been driving for four hours when the accident took place. If I hadn't been half asleep and had been concentrating I'm sure that I could have avoided her car without crashing."

The letter was stolen from a file in Eric's office by a friend of Amanda's who works for Eric.

Consider whether:

(a) Jack may successfully assert that Amanda is estopped from denying Jack's allegation of negligence in consequence of the successful claim for negligence which Tom brought against her;

(b) Amanda's conviction will be admissible in evidence for Jack;

(c) If Amanda asserts that Jack and she were equally to blame for the accident, she will bear the burden of proving this and, if so, to what standard;

(d) Amanda can call Mr Smith, the mechanic who maintains her car, to state in court that he examined the car after the accident and that, in his opinion, the steering had probably failed before she crashed into Tom;

(e) Jack can prevent Amanda from adducing in evidence the letter which he wrote to his solicitor.

Answer

(a) Neither a cause of action estoppel nor an issue estoppel can arise in these circumstances for two reasons.

First, in order for an estoppel by record to arise, the parties to the latter proceedings must be the parties to the former proceedings or their privies. Here, however (as in *Townsend v Bishop*), the parties are different (Tom and Amanda being the parties to the first proceedings and Jack and Amanda being the parties to the second).

Secondly, in order for an estoppel by record to arise the cause of action or issue which is being litigated in the latter proceedings must have been determined in the former proceedings (see, for example, *Brunsden v Humphrey*). Here, however, neither the cause of action nor any issue which Jack and Amanda are litigating were determined in the proceedings between Tom and Amanda (the first proceedings determining that Amanda was to blame for the collision in which Tom's car was damaged, the second concerning her liability with regard to the damage to Jack's car when it left the road).

(b) Amanda's conviction for dangerous driving appears to be of relevance in determining whether she was negligent in the context of the claim brought by Jack. Consequently, the conviction appears to be admissible under s.11 of the Civil Evidence Act 1968. Under s.11, Amanda will be taken to have committed the offence unless she proves to the civil standard of proof that she did not commit it (*McCauley v Hope*). It is unclear, though, whether, if Amanda asserts that she did not commit the offence, the conviction amounts to evidence to the effect that she did (*Stupple v Royal Insurance Co Ltd*). It appears, however, that proving that she did not commit the offence will be a difficult task (*Hunter v Chief Constable of the West Midlands Police*).

(c) The party who raises an issue in civil proceedings is required to prove it (see, for example, *Wakelin v London and South Western Railway*). Jack, the claimant, bears the burden of proving those issues which he has raised (essentially, that Amanda owed him a duty of care, that her conduct amounted to a breach of that duty and that, in consequence of her breach of duty, he suffered loss). Amanda, the defendant, bears the burden of proving those issues which she raises (though she bears no burden of proof merely because she denies assertions made by Jack). Thus, since Amanda raises the issue of whether Jack is partly to blame for the damage which he suffered, the burden of proof in relation to the defence of contributory negligence lies on her.

The requisite standard of proof in civil proceedings is proof on a balance of probabilities. Thus, in order to establish her defence, Amanda must essentially persuade the judge that it is more probable than not that Jack's negligence was a contributory cause of his accident (*Miller v Minister of Pensions*).

(d) Expert opinion evidence is only admissible in relation to an issue where the court requires the assistance of an expert in order to determine that issue (see, for example, *R. v Smith*).

[*Note:* in civil prceedings the evidence is admissible under s.3(1) of the Civil Evidence Act 1972; in criminal proceedings it would be admissible at common law.]

It would appear that a judge would require the opinion of an expert witness in order to determine whether Amanda's steering had failed prior to the accident. Thus, it appears that expert evidence is admissible in this context.

Further, a witness is only competent (or "qualified", to adopt the words of s.3(1) of the Civil Evidence Act 1972) to give expert evidence if he is an expert. Formal training and/or qualifications are not required provided that the witness has obtained the necessary expertise (see, for example, *R. v Stockwell*). If the judge is satisfied that Mr Smith is competent (*i.e.* qualified) to give expert evidence on this issue then he may receive his evidence.

It should be noted, however, that the Civil Procedure Rules 1998 give a judge in civil proceedings powers to exclude, limit or determine the nature of otherwise admissible expert evidence which a judge in criminal proceedings does not possess. Thus, this being a civil trial, under Part 35 of the Civil Procedure Rules 1998, the court's permission is required either to call an expert witness or to put his report in evidence, the court being required to restrict expert evidence to that which is reasonably required to resolve the proceedings. Further, this being a civil trial, if the court gives Amanda permission to adduce Mr Smith's evidence, it is probable that his evidence will be given by written report and that Amanda will not be permitted to call Mr Smith to give oral evidence. Moreover, under Part 35 of the Civil Procedure Rules 1998, the court may direct that the expert evidence in relation to the issue be given by a single joint expert, in which case the claimant may not be prepared to agree Mr Smith as a suitable single joint expert.

If Amanda is permitted to adduce Mr Smith's evidence, he must be aware of the fact that, under the Civil Procedure Rules 1998, his duty to the court overrides his duty to Amanda. His report must state that he understands this duty, has complied with it and will continue to do so. The report must, as required by Part 35 of the Civil Procedure Rules 1998, amongst other things, specify the expert's qualifications, the literature etc., which he relied upon when making the report, and his conclusions, it must summarise his instructions and must be verified by a "statement of truth". If a range of expert opinions exist in relation to the matter which the report concerns, the report must summarise these and must indicate why Mr Smith formed his opinion. The report must summarise the expert's conclusions and, if the expert's opinion is a qualified opinion, it must state the nature of the qualification.

If the court does not direct the use of a single joint expert, it will probably direct the parties to exchange expert reports simultaneously on a specified day. If Amanda fails to disclose Mr Smith's report then, under Part 35 of the Civil Procedure Rules 1998, Amanda will only be able to rely upon the report or to call Mr Smith at the trial with the court's permission.

Finally, when Mr Smith's report is served on Jack, Jack will, within 28 days, again under Part 35 of the Civil Procedure Rules 1995, be entitled to put written questions about the report to the Mr Smith for the purpose of clarifying it. Mr Smith's answers will be treated as part of the report. If Mr Smith does not provide answers, the court may direct that Amanda cannot rely on his evidence.

(e) The statement contained in the letter written by Jack to his solicitor is a hearsay statement because it was not made in oral evidence in the proceedings between Jack and Amanda and is tendered as evidence of the matters stated (*i.e.* it is relied upon to prove that Jack was partly to blame for the damage which he suffered) (see Civil Evidence Act 1995, s.1). Whilst the statement is an informal admission, such statements no longer fall within a preserved common law exception to the hearsay rule (Civil Evidence Act 1995, s.7). The statement will, however, fall within the general exception to the hearsay rule contained in s.1 of the 1995 Act. In relation to this hearsay evidence, Amanda should comply with the notice requirements imposed by s.2(1) of the Civil Evidence Act 1998 and CPR 33.2. Since the hearsay evidence is not contained in a witness statement, it appears that this will require Amanda to serve a notice on Jack identifying the hearsay evidence, stating that she intends to rely on it and giving the reason why Jack will not be called by her. If Amanda fails to comply with these notice requirements this will not affect the admissibility of the hearsay evidence but may reduce its weight and may have costs and/or adjournment implications. Amanda may make use either of the original letter or of a copy (authenticated in a manner approved by the court) in order to prove the statement (s.8). In the circumstances (see s.4), the evidential weight of the statement will probably be high (it is unlikely that the claimant would flippantly make such a statement adverse to his interests).

Section 1 of the 1995 Act does not make a hearsay statement admissible if it was excluded by some rule of evidence other than the rule against hearsay (*e.g.* the opinion evidence rule). Whilst Jack's statement is opinion evidence, s.3(2) of the Civil Evidence Act 1972 makes non-expert opinion evidence admissible, even in relation to an ultimate issue, to prove facts which a witness personally perceived.

A communication in confidence between a client and his legal adviser for the purpose of obtaining or giving legal advice is subject to legal professional privilege in the form of "legal advice privilege" (*Balabel v Air India*). In order for legal advice privilege to arise, however, the advice must take place in a "relevant legal context" (*e.g.* some forms of business advice given by solicitors may not be privileged) (*Three Rivers DC v Governors and Company of the Bank of England (No.6)*). Thus, upon the assumption that Jack wrote the letter for the purpose of obtaining legal advice, had the letter not fallen into Amanda's possession, Jack could have refused to produce it or to answer questions concerning its contents and could require his solicitor to do the same. Since the letter has fallen into Amanda's hands, however, she will be able to adduce it in evidence unless Jack obtains an injunction ordering her to return the letter to him. Further, if she has made copies of the letter, the injunction will prevent her from using the copies as secondary evidence of the letter's contents in the course of the proceedings between Jack and herself (see *Calcraft v Guest* and *Lord Ashburton v Pape*). If the letter has already been adduced in evidence then Jack will be too late to obtain an injunction (*Goddard v Nationwide Building Society*). Moreover, the court may refuse to grant him an injunction in the exercise of its equitable discretion (*e.g.* if there has been undue delay in applying for it) (*Goddard v Nationwide Building Society*).

INDEX

LEGAL TAXONOMY

FROM SWEET & MAXWELL

This index has been prepared using Sweet and Maxwell's Legal Taxonomy. Main index entries conform to keywords provided by the Legal Taxonomy except where references to specific documents or non-standard terms (denoted by quotation marks) have been included. These keywords provide a means of identifying similar concepts in other Sweet & Maxwell publications and online services to which keywords from the Legal Taxonomy have been applied. Readers may find some minor differences between terms used in the text and those which appear in the index. Suggestions to *taxonomy@sweetandmaxwell.co.uk*.

(All references are to page number)